Bloom's
GUIDES

Kate Chopin's
The Awakening

The Adventures of Huckleberry Finn

All the Pretty Horses

Animal Farm

The Autobiography of Malcolm X

The Awakening

Beloved

Beowulf

Brave New World

The Canterbury Tales

The Catcher in the Rye

The Chosen

The Crucible

Cry, the Beloved Country

Death of a Salesman

Fahrenheit 451

Frankenstein

The Glass Menagerie

The Grapes of Wrath

Great Expectations

The Great Gatsby

Hamlet

The Handmaid's Tale

The House on Mango Street

I Know Why the Caged Bird Sings

The Iliad

Invisible Man

Jane Eyre

Lord of the Flies

Macbeth

Maggie: A Girl of the Streets

The Member of the Wedding

The Metamorphosis

Native Son

1984

The Odyssey

Oedipus Rex

Of Mice and Men

One Hundred Years of Solitude

Pride and Prejudice

Ragtime

The Red Badge of Courage

Romeo and Juliet

The Scarlet Letter

A Separate Peace

Slaughterhouse-Five

Snow Falling on Cedars

The Stranger

A Streetcar Named Desire

The Sun Also Rises

A Tale of Two Cities

The Things They Carried

To Kill a Mockingbird

Uncle Tom's Cabin

The Waste Land

Wuthering Heights

Bloom's

GUIDES

Kate Chopin's
The Awakening

Edited & with an Introduction
by Harold Bloom

BLOOM'S
LITERARY CRITICISM
An imprint of Infobase Publishing

Bloom's Guides: The Awakening

Copyright © 2008 by Infobase Publishing

Introduction © 2008 by Harold Bloom

Bloom's Literary Criticism
An imprint of Infobase Publishing
132 West 31st Street
New York, NY 10001

Library of Congress Cataloging-in-Publication Data
Chopin, Kate, 1851–1904.
  Kate Chopin's The awakening / [edited and introduction by] Harold Bloom.
     p. cm. — (Bloom's guides)
  Includes bibliographical references and index.
  ISBN 978-0-7910-9791-5 (hardcover)
  1. Chopin, Kate, 1851–1904. Awakening. 2. New Orleans (La.)—In literature. 3. Sex role in literature. 4. Women in literature. I. Bloom, Harold. II. Title. III. Title: Awakening. IV. Series.

  PS1294.C63A64345 2008
  813'.4—dc22

2007047408

Contributing Editor: Portia Williams Weiskel
Cover design by Takeshi Takahashi
Printed in the United States of America
Bang EJB 10 9 8 7 6 5 4 3 2 1
This book is printed on acid-free paper.

Contents

Introduction

HAROLD BLOOM

There are several intrinsic affinities between Walt Whitman's poetry and *The Awakening*, which I will explore here. However, there is an ironical extrinsic similarity that I mention first, doubtless at some risk of giving offense. Whitman's poetry is now much written about by academic critics who care only for the homoerotic Walt; the poetry, to them, is of interest only insofar as it represents the poet's undoubted desires. Similarly, Kate Chopin's *The Awakening* is now a favorite work of feminist critics, who find in it a forerunner of Liberation. I regard all this with amiable irony, since so much of Whitman's best poetry is quite overtly autoerotic while Edna Pontellier's awakening is to her own "shifting, treacherous, fickle deeps," not so much of her soul (as Chopin carefully adds) but of her body. If *The Awakening* is a breakthrough, it is as the subtle female version of the self-gratification slyly celebrated by Goethe (in *Faust, Part Two*) and openly sung by Walt Whitman.

Though *The Awakening* follows in the path of Flaubert's *Madame Bovary*, it shares little with that formidable precursor. Emma Bovary indeed awakens, belatedly and tragically, but the narcissistic Edna singly drifts from one mode of reverie to another, until she drowns herself in the sea, which for her as for Whitman represents night and the mother, death and the inmost self. Far from being a rebel, moved by sympathy with victims of societal oppression, Edna is even more isolated at the end than before. It is a very peculiar academic fashion that has transformed Edna into any kind of a feminist heroine. The protagonist of *The Awakening* is her own victim, unless one agrees with Kathleen Margaret Lane's assertion that: "Edna awakens to the horrible knowledge that she can never, because she is female, be her own person." Late nineteenth-century Creole society was not Afghanistan under the rule of the Taliban. Chopin shows it as having something of a hothouse atmosphere, but that alas does seem the only possible context for Edna, who in fact loves no one—not her children, husband, friends, or lovers—and whose awakening is only to the ecstasies of self-gratification.

The influence of Whitman is pervasive throughout *The Awakening*, and suggests that Chopin was deeply immersed in *Leaves of Grass*, particularly in the *Sea-Drift* poems, and in the *Lilacs* elegy for Lincoln. Gouvernail, the benign bachelor who is one of the guests at Edna's birthday party, had appeared earlier in Chopin's short story, "A Respectable Woman," where he recites part of Section 21 of *Song of Myself*: "Night of south winds—night of the large few stars!/Still nodding night—." The entire passage could serve as an epigraph for *The Awakening*.

> Press close bare-bosom'd night—press close magnetic
> nourishing night!
> Night of south winds—night of the few large stars!
> Still nodding night—mad naked summer night.

This is the model for the ecstatic rebirth of Edna's self, a narcissistic self-investment that awards Edna a new ego. Had Edna been able to see that her awakening was to a passion for herself, then her suicide perhaps could have been avoided. Chopin, a very uneven stylist, nevertheless was erotically subtler than most of her critics have been. Edna emulates Whitman by falling in love with her own body: "observing closely, as if it were something she saw for the first time, the fine, firm quality and texture of her flesh." This stems from Whitman's grand proclamation: "If I worship one thing more than another it shall be the spread of my own body, or any part of it." When Edna awakens to self, she hears the voice of the sea, and experiences its Whitmanesque embrace: "The touch of the sea is sensuous, enfolding the body in its soft, close embrace." When the naked Edna enters the mothering sea for a last time, we hear an echo of the undulating serpentine death that Whitman welcomes in

When Lilacs Last in the Dooryard Bloom'd: "The foamy wavelets curled up to her white feet and coiled like serpents about her ankles." Is this indeed a chant of Women's Liberation, or a siren song of a Whitmanesque Love-Death?

Biographical Sketch

Kate Chopin was born Katherine O'Flaherty in St. Louis, Missouri, on February 8, 1851. Her father, Thomas O'Flaherty, was an Irish immigrant who became a prosperous merchant before his death in a railway accident in 1855. Her mother, Eliza Faris, was descended from French Creole aristocrats. Chopin attended the St. Louis Academy of the Sacred Heart, where she read copiously, learned to play the piano, became fluent in French, and passionately supported the Confederacy during the Civil War. Chopin became more interested in literature and storytelling after the deaths of her father, great-grandmother, and half-brother during these years. She graduated from the academy in 1868 and became a belle in St. Louis high society. She soon became aware of feminist social issues and became rebellious, complaining of the parties a belle was expected to attend, and of the young men at dances whose "only talent" resided in their feet. She began to smoke cigarettes and wrote a feminist fable, "Emancipation." She read and admired the works of Jane Austen, the Brontë sisters, George Eliot, and George Sand.

In 1870 she married Oscar Chopin, a twenty-five-year-old cotton trader, New Orleans native, and Creole. They lived first in New Orleans and then, with the failure of Chopin's business in 1879, on a plantation at a place called La Cote Joyeuse. During her marriage she was an exemplary wife; according to her daughter, the "Lady Bountiful of the neighborhood," known as an engaging personality. During her marriage, Chopin explored New Orleans on foot and by streetcar, writing about what she saw, attending the theater and the opera, and spending her vacations engaged in reading at Grand Isle on the Gulf of Mexico, where *The Awakening* is set. After Oscar Chopin died of swamp fever in 1882, she returned, with her six children, to St. Louis and began to write sketches of Louisiana life for publication. In 1899 her first published poem, "If It Might Be," appeared in the magazine *America*. During the 1890s Chopin wrote more than one hundred short stories and hosted a salon in her home at 3317 Morgan Street. Her articles, poems, and stories were published in *Atlantic Monthly, Criterion, Harper's Young People, Vogue,* and the *St. Louis Post-Dispatch.* Her books include *At Fault* (1890), *Bayou Folk* (1894), and *A Night at Acadie* (1897). In 1899 Chopin published her final novella, *The Awakening.* The book caused a critical furor that ended her literary career. The public condemned her candid treatment of a young married woman's sexual and spiritual awakening.

Kate Chopin died from a cerebral hemorrhage, on August 22, 1904, after spending the day at the world's fair in St. Louis.

The Story Behind the Story

Few novels can compete with *The Awakening* for generating critical responses so diverse as to seem uninspired by the same books. Published in Chicago in 1899 by Herbert Stone & Co. and selling for $1.50 a copy, the novel received the critical attention appropriately due a writer already acclaimed for her successful short stories.

At one extreme was the prepublication commentary of Lucy Monroe, a reviewer for the publisher, who praised the author's literary brilliance and promised that the novel would leave the reader with "the impression of being at the very heart of things" (*Norton Critical Edition: The Awakening*, 1994, 161). Another reviewer reacted as if she had been personally damaged by the novel's effect: "One would fain beg the gods . . . for sleep unending rather than to know what an ugly, cruel, loathsome monster Passion can be when . . . it . . . finally awakens" (Frances Porcher, ibid, 162). The *St. Louis Post-Dispatch* (May 20, 1899) praised the "complete mastery . . . apparent on every page" and empathized with the heroine whose husband regarded her "as a bit of decorative furniture" (ibid, 164). The *Chicago Times-Herald* (June 1, 1899) dismissed the book as "sex fiction" (ibid, 166).

Within these extremes was a range of mixed responses, generally more positive about Chopin's writing skills and more negative to the point of disgust and alarm about the character and behavior of her heroine. One novel reaction deserves special mention: Writing in 1909, Percival Pollard presumptuously claimed that Edna was not a credible human being. The issue of Edna's relative "awakeness," he opined, "would be an interesting question for students of sleep-walking"; later he escalated his disdain with this mocking tone: "Ah, these married women, who have never, by some strange chance, had the flaming torch applied, how they do flash out when the right moment comes!" (*Their Day in Court*, Neale Publishing, 41–45).

Although friends and many readers rallied in her support, Kate Chopin was troubled by the novel's unequal reception and dismayed by the damage it brought to her reputation. In the July 1899 edition of *Book News* she offered a tongue-in-cheek defense of her heroine:

> I never dreamed of Mrs. Pontellier making such a mess of things and working out her own damnation as she did. If I had had the slightest intimation of such a thing [,] I would have excluded her from the company. But when I found out what she was up to, the play was half over and it was then too late. (Quoted in *Critical Essays on Kate Chopin*, Alice Hall Petry, ed., G. K. Hall & Co., 11.)

What resources did Kate Chopin draw upon to have so confidentially and clairvoyantly presented this betrayal of a woman in existential crisis and then not retract it after hearing her heroine maligned and disbelieved by so many? No evidence exists suggesting the story was autobiographical. After her husband died early and unexpectedly in 1882, she began her writing career, became a prominent member of the social and literary circles in St. Louis, and was rumored to have enjoyed a romantic fling with a younger male resembling her character Alcée Arobin. In 1894 she wrote:

> If it were possible for my husband . . . to come back to earth, I feel that I would unhesitatingly give up everything that has come into my life since [then] . . . and join my existence again with [his]. (Quoted in Toth, *Unveiling*, 162.)

Biographers tell us that Chopin descended from eccentric and strong-willed women. She certainly displayed wit and imaginative thinking. To the question—Is Love Divine?—asked of prominent women by the *St. Louis Post-Dispatch* in 1898, Chopin, a true novelist, gave an unconventional response highlighting the mysteries of love:

It is as difficult to distinguish between the divine love and the natural, animal love, as it is to explain just why we love at all. (Quoted in Walker, *Kate Chopin*, 2001, 114)

Another clue to Chopin's (and Edna's) sensibility is a remark the author recorded in which she vows never to "fall into the useless degrading life of most married ladies" (*Kate Chopin's Personal Papers*, eds. Toth and Seyersted, 1998, 102).

Chopin conceived of Edna's story during the decade of Darwin and Huxley, Elizabeth Cady Stanton and Susan B. Anthony (and other "uppity women")—all in their way challenging the notion of a fixed and final truth. But despite these encouraging influences, the prevailing Victorian code for female behavior was too entrenched to condone a "shocking" display of female eroticism or to give center stage to a woman in the throes of self-liberation. After the first rush of attention and commentary, the novel went out of print. Chopin scholar Emily Toth has debunked the persistent myth that the book had been banned from the St. Louis library, but it did fall into such obscurity that it was not listed in Robert Spiller's 1948 edition of the *Literary History of the United States*, although other Chopin works were included.

French scholar Cyrille Arnavon's 1953 translation of *The Awakening* and Per Seyersted's 1969 biography revived interest in Chopin and her novel. The feminist movement in the sixties elevated Chopin's stature; since then, her work has achieved its prominent place in the American literature canon.

Published at the turn of the century, *The Awakening* is a fictional embodiment of the struggles that were ahead for women. Chopin scholar Joyce Dyer writes:

Chopin decides there will be no easy answers for Edna, just as there would be no easy answers for the women of the twentieth century who followed her. (*The Awakening: A Novel of Beginnings*, 1993, 17)

Showing how far appreciation of Chopin has come, Peggy Skaggs praises *The Awakening* for demonstrating "that unless one's inner person is integral with one's outer roles and relationships a fully satisfying life cannot be achieved" (*Kate Chopin*, Twayne's, Indiana University, Bloomington, 1985).

List of Characters

Edna Pontellier, twenty-eight years old, is more handsome than beautiful, her face "captivating by reason of a certain frankness of expression and a contradictory subtle play of features." She is the daughter of a Civil War colonel of the Confederate Army, raised in Kentucky and married, perversely because of her family's protests, to a Creole New Orleans businessman, Léonce Pontellier. Her Protestant reserve contrasts with the risqué familiarity present in the conversations of the married women in the Creole summer colony. Edna is without artifice and given to moments of "caprice," such as swimming beyond what others consider a safe distance from shore, acts that reflect her dissatisfaction with her unexamined, interior life. She is an "engaging" personality, neither very talented nor intellectually curious, and disinterested in Creole or any other domestic habits. In the space of a few months, she "awakens" to her "true" self. Hers is the "awakening" of an ordinary woman to love, the sensuous world, and her own spirituality. The ambiance of this social milieu at Grand Isle invites her to "loosen . . . the mantle of reserve that [has] always enveloped her," but Edna does not understand the rules of Creole society which, although they allow for the language of personal freedom, demand as strict a propriety as any in the North. Hedonism, the pursuit of pleasure for its own sake, shapes her self-discovery, with disastrous results.

Léonce Pontellier is Edna's husband. He is forty-one years old, a slender, nearsighted Creole with a slight stoop. A prosperous New Orleans businessman, he is conventional, snobbish, kind, and generous to his wife and children, though emotionally remote. Edna's marriage to Léonce "was purely an accident, in this respect resembling many other marriages which masquerade as the decrees of Fate." In her inexperience and infatuation she had mistaken the flattery of his devotion for a "sympathy of thought and taste between them." Her Protestant family violently opposed her marriage to a Catholic which, the narrator tells us, was enough to ensure that she would marry him as quickly as possible. Léonce values Edna as he does all of his finest possessions.

Raoul and **Etienne** are Edna's two young sons. They interest her in "an uneven, impulsive way. . . . [S]he would sometimes forget them" entirely. Because they are in the constant company of their nursemaid, they cause no trouble and come to no harm, despite Edna's indifference.

Robert Lebrun is the instrument of Edna's "awakening" and the focus of her passion. The twenty-six-year-old son of Madame Lebrun, he devotes himself each summer to a young woman, widow, or married guest at Grand Isle, the summer colony on the Gulf of Mexico owned by his family. He is charming, idle, and in love with Edna Pontellier. Early one evening they enjoy a swim, and Edna becomes aware of a "certain light [dawning] dimly within her,—the light which, showing the way, forbids it." He travels to Mexico in order to end their love affair; his reunion with Edna, after his return, seems to fulfill her newly awakened desire. When he abandons her, she commits suicide.

Alcée Arobin is a sophisticated and accomplished escort for respectable, married New Orleans women of Edna's background. He frequently accompanies Edna to the horse races and to dinner when Léonce is away on business. Alcée's character both mirrors and contrasts Robert Lebrun. While Robert is in Mexico and Léonce is in New York, Edna succumbs to Arobin's practiced manner and approach. While he is attracted to Edna and not ungentlemanly in his conduct, his sensuous nature awakens the sexual passions she had previously focused on Robert. Her feelings for Arobin confuse her and finally convince her that, without Robert, she will be only promiscuous.

Madame Adèle Ratignolle has been married seven years, has three children, talks constantly of her "condition," and has a fondness for candy. She has perfect hands. Edna, with her "sensuous susceptibility to beauty," is attracted by the physical charm and the personality of this Creole woman. She is a shrewd judge of the risks Edna takes in her affair with Robert and in the appearance of an attachment to Alcée Arobin. In many ways, she acts as Edna's best friend. Edna often visits the Ratignolles' apartment, above their prosperous drugstore.

Mademoiselle Reisz is an elderly concert pianist. She is a single, disagreeable woman with no family and few friends. She is one representation of the life possible for an independent woman in 1899. While a guest at Grand Isle, she develops a friendship with Edna and Robert. When Robert is in Mexico, he writes letters to her about his love for Edna. Edna visits her apartment in New Orleans to read these letters from Robert.

Madame Lebrun is the mother of Robert and Victor. Grand Isle had been the luxury summer property of the Lebrun family. Madame Lebrun maintains her comfortable life by renting cottages to "exclusive visitors from the 'Quartier Francais'." Her efficiency and charm symbolize bourgeois Creole resourcefulness and respectability.

The Colonel is Edna Pontellier's father. He had been an officer in the Confederate Army and is still known by his military title. He is gruff and opinionated, but he loves his daughter. On a visit to New Orleans to buy a wedding gift for another daughter, he advises Léonce to be more firm with Edna, to allow her less freedom to neglect her domestic duties. Edna is happy to see him return to his Mississippi plantation.

Victor Lebrun is Robert's nineteen-year-old brother. He is youthfully infatuated with Edna, probably in response to the love his older brother feels for her. He is the last person to see Edna, at Grand Isle, before her suicide.

Doctor Mandelet is the kindly, paternal, and weary family physician to the Pontelliers and the Ratignolles. As an observer in the story, he notes both her sad confusion and her ebullient charm. What he cannot understand, as Chopin illustrates, is that Edna's, or any woman's, dissatisfactions are rooted outside stereotypes of mental weakness. Although he is well-meaning, the good doctor is of little use to his female patients.

Mrs. Merriman and **Mrs. Highcamp** are acquaintances of Edna's in New Orleans. They function as stock characters in the story. They enjoy parties and horse racing in the company of Alcée Arobin, all the while maintaining their respectability as married women. Their names are reminiscent of characters in a late-seventeenth-century comedy of manners.

Summary and Analysis

Kate Chopin's *The Awakening*, published in 1899, caused a critical furor that ended her literary career. Readers were shocked not only by the portrayal of a young woman in rebellion against her husband, but also by the novella's frank treatment of sexuality and the protagonist's love for a younger man. Most of this short tale is told from the point of view of Edna Pontellier, the young wife, with the narrator providing occasional clarification. The effect of this limited point of view is impressionistic; that is, it presents subjective impressions rather than objective reality. The most prominent motif, or recurring thematic element, is of "awakening," an idea whose representation punctuates the novella.

In **chapter one**, Léonce Pontellier is at the summer colony of Grand Isle to visit his wife and two children for the weekend. He departs for the evening to spend time gambling and socializing with other men of his class, leaving Edna in the company of young Robert Lebrun. The "utter nonsense" of the conversation between Lebrun and Mrs. Pontellier bores him. Mr. Pontellier is a study in both complacency and impatience: Edna returns from the beach with a sunburn and he is disturbed that this "valuable piece of personal property [had] suffered some damage." He views Edna as his property and is comfortable with that relationship.

The atmosphere is languorous on the porch where Robert Lebrun and Edna Pontellier sit and talk during the summer afternoon (**chapter two**). They are well matched, both young and eager to talk about themselves, yet interested in each other's stories.

The "awakening" motif first surfaces in **chapter three**, when Mr. Pontellier returns from dinner late in the evening and wakes Edna to tell her "anecdotes and bits of news and gossip that he had gathered during the day." He is discouraged that his wife, "the sole object of his existence," is too tired to be interested. In "a monotonous, insistent way" he reproaches Edna for her "habitual neglect of the children," claiming that one of the sleeping boys has a fever. She refuses to respond to her husband's interrogation; he finishes his cigar and falls asleep immediately. But Edna is wide awake. The contrast between the "tacit and self-understood" kindness of her husband and the "indescribable oppression" of their marriage "fill[s] her whole being with a vague anguish."

Chapter four focuses on Mr. Pontellier's vague dissatisfaction with his wife: "It was something which he felt rather than perceived, and he never voiced the feeling without subsequent regret and ample atonement," as displayed in **chapter three**. Edna is not a "mother-woman," like the others who summer at Grand Isle, those who "idolized their children, worshipped their husbands, and esteemed it a holy privilege to efface themselves as individuals and grow wings as ministering angels." The tone of this description is both the sarcastic observation of the narrator and the heartfelt sentiment of Mr. Pontellier. Madame Ratignolle is one such woman whom Léonce Pontellier deems "the embodiment of every womanly grace and charm." Frankness and familiarity, or "freedom of expression," are characteristic of the conversations conducted among the summer colony guests but alien to Edna's northern background. Vivid in her memory is the shock of hearing Madame Ratignolle relate the "harrowing story of one of her *accouchements*" (birthings) to a male guest. A narrative tension, or conflict, develops throughout the story between Edna's habitual reserve and the "freedom of expression" of the Creole culture into which she has married. This tension foreshadows and constructs the terms of her suicide.

Robert Lebrun's position in the summer colony society is clarified in **chapter five**. Each summer he attaches himself to a woman guest—usually married—that he fancies. This summer he is the "devoted attendant" of Mrs. Pontellier. They share an "advanced stage of intimacy and camaraderie," sitting among the women on the porch on the summer afternoon. With mock seriousness, Robert mournfully comments on Madame Ratignolle's cold cruelty to one who had adored her the summer before. She recalls that he was "a troublesome cat," while he compares himself to "an adoring dog." More to the point, she claims that her husband might have become jealous. All laugh because, as both the narrator and Edna understand, "the Creole husband is never jealous; with him the gangrene passion . . . has become dwarfed by disuse." Edna sketches Madame Ratignolle, who is "seated there like some sensuous Madonna, with the gleam of the fading day enriching her splendid color." As a likeness, her portrait of Madame Ratignolle is a failure, and Edna crumples it in her hands, an act significant in two ways. Her work emerges as untutored and inept. The act also suggests that, although the likeness fails in one sense, in another way the work may have succeeded as an impressionistic image. As yet, Edna has no knowledge or referents by which to define either her art or herself.

Chapter six is a brief psychological sketch of Edna's moment of awakening to "her position in the universe as a human being, [recognizing] her relations as an individual to the world within and about her." She is twenty-eight years old and at "the beginning of things." The "voice of the sea" is seductive to her, its touch like a "sensuous . . . close embrace." This is a disturbing and dangerous point for Edna, and her "contradictory impulses" mirror the contradictory outcomes possible from this place of beginning: She may gain wisdom, or she may perish.

Edna's relationship with Adèle Ratignolle is the subject of **chapter seven**. Edna, with her "sensuous susceptibility to beauty" is attracted by the physical charm and personality of this Creole woman. In the heat of the afternoon, they sit together on the beach, Edna fanning her companion and contemplatively watching the sea. Adèle asks what she is thinking, and Edna makes an effort to respond to what is only a rhetorical question. Adèle protests that it is "really too hot to think, especially to think about thinking." Edna confides in Madame Ratignolle that the sea reminds her of herself as a young girl, "walking through the green meadow again; idly, aimlessly, unthinking and unguided." Like a "first breath of freedom" Edna feels "intoxicated" as she reveals a small portion of her feelings to Madame Ratignolle. Adèle seems sympathetic, holding Edna's hand "firmly and warmly" and stroking it "fondly." The physical affection startles Edna, who is unaccustomed to such displays of warmth. Her girlhood infatuations with young men had been distant, cerebral; her friendships with women have been earnest, her female acquaintances as "self-contained" as she. On her desk is a framed picture of an actor, a tragedian, which she sometimes kisses passionately when alone.

Madame Ratignolle warns Robert of a potential threat or danger she perceives in Edna (**chapter eight**): "She is not one of us; she is not like us. She might make the unfortunate blunder of taking you seriously." Chastened by this warning, Robert assures Madame Ratignolle that there is "no earthly possibility" Edna Pontellier will ever take him seriously. Impressionistic authorial intrusions describe the atmosphere of the scene, as in the satirical description of Madame Lebrun at her sewing machine: "A little black girl sat on the floor, and with her hands worked the treadle of the machine. The Creole woman does not take any chances which may be avoided of imperiling her health."

A few weeks after Robert's conversation with Madame Ratignolle, the families gather for dinner and casual entertainment (**chapter nine**). The scene is hectic and the atmosphere domestic and indulgent. After the children are sent to bed, Robert asks Edna if she would like to hear Mademoiselle Reisz play the piano. The introduction of this character, a well-known concert pianist and a guest with whom Edna is apparently acquainted, emphasizes Edna's self-containment and the reader's always limited knowledge of her. Mademoiselle Reisz agrees to play for the guests only because she likes Edna. We know only that Edna is "very fond of music" and that she "sometimes liked to sit in the room of mornings when Madame Ratignolle played or practiced." How this has earned Mademoiselle Reisz's affection remains a mystery. Edna is deeply affected by Mademoiselle Reisz's artistry. Although it "was not the first time she had heard an artist at the piano [p]erhaps it was the first time she was ready, perhaps the first time her being was tempered to take an impress of the abiding truth." The meaning of this may seem as obscure to the reader as it is to Edna.

After the party the Pontelliers, the Ratignolles, and Robert Lebrun walk to the beach for a late-night swim (**chapter ten**). Edna has been taking swimming instruction all summer, without success. The water has terrified her, until now. On this evening, she swims "like a little tottering, stumbling, clutching child, who of a sudden realizes its powers, and walks for the first time alone, boldly and with over-confidence." She has a sudden desire to swim "far out, where no woman had swum before." The "space and solitude" of the gulf seem to enchant her, offering a place in which she might lose or transcend herself. For a moment, she is terrified by a "quick vision of death" that seems to kill her "soul." Afterward, she walks back to the house alone. Madame Lebrun later remarks to Mr. Pontellier that his wife seems "capricious." He agrees that she is, but only "sometimes, not often."

Robert overtakes Edna and she confides in him that this night has seemed "like a night in a dream," that "[t]here must be spirits abroad to-night." Robert whispers to her that there are indeed spirits abroad, that on this date, at this time, "a spirit that has haunted these shores for ages rises up from the Gulf. . . . [to] seek one mortal to hold him company . . . [and] to-night he found Mrs. Pontellier." Edna is wounded by his banter, but "he could not tell her that he had penetrated her mood and understood." They reach the house where Edna rests in a hammock. Robert sits on the stairs near her and smokes a cigarette. Neither speak, but both are moved by the "first-felt throbbings of desire."

In **chapter eleven**, an incident occurs between Mr. and Mrs. Pontellier that mirrors and contrasts the scene of companionable silence between Edna and Robert that marked the preceding chapter. The motif of awakening is thus juxtaposed with the power of unconsciousness, represented by the overwhelming need for sleep. Edna refuses to leave the hammock and come to bed, as her husband insists. She recognizes that "her will had blazed up, stubborn and resistant," but at the same time, she feels "like one who awakens gradually out of a dream, a delicious, grotesque, impossible dream, to feel again the realities pressing into her soul." Léonce draws up a rocker near her and smokes a cigar. At last overcome by the need for sleep, Edna enters the house, pausing to ask her husband if he will follow. "Just as soon as I have finished my cigar," he responds.

After a "troubled and feverish sleep" Edna wakes early, moved by vague impulses, "as if she had placed herself in alien hands for direction, and freed her soul of responsibility." Impressionistic images of the day heighten the effect of Edna's disturbing dreams. Lovers stroll to meet the boat to the *Chênière Caminada*, to attend Mass. A "lady in black, with her Sunday prayer-book, velvet and gold-clasped, and her Sunday silver beads" follows them. Monsieur Farival, in a straw hat, follows the lady in black, and a "young barefooted Spanish girl, with a red kerchief and a basket, follows Monsieur Farival." The "little negro girl who worked Madame Lebrun's sewing-machine" sweeps the gallery; Edna sends the girl to awaken Robert, to tell him to meet her. She has never requested his presence before; she "had never seemed to want him before." Mariequita, the Spanish girl, jealously asks Robert if Mrs. Pontellier is his "sweetheart." She is unimpressed to learn that she is "a married lady, and has two children." She knows of a man who ran away with another man's wife.

Edna finds the atmosphere of the church at *Chênière Caminada* oppressive (**chapter thirteen**). She leaves the Mass, and Robert follows her, provoking some gossip among those who remain. He takes her to rest at the cottage of Madame Antoine. Sensuous images convey connotations of beauty and strangeness: "the voice of the sea whispering through the reeds," a "jagged fence made of sea-drift," a "mild-faced Acadian" boy draws water for her that is "cool to her heated face." She notices, for the first time, the "fine, firm quality and texture of her flesh." She sleeps and wakes refreshed and "very hungry." She tears a piece of bread from a loaf "with her strong, white teeth" and downs a glass of wine. She goes "softly out of doors," plucks an orange from a tree, and tosses it at Robert, who did not know that she had awakened. The rest of the party had returned to Grand Isle hours before, but Robert reassures her that Léonce will not worry, since "he knows you are with me." As night commences, Edna and Robert sit in the grass as Madame Antoine tells them stories. Symbols of the world they have left behind and harbingers of the choice Edna will make for herself, the shadows "lengthened and crept out like stealthy, grotesque monsters across the grass."

On their return from *Chênière Caminada* (**chapter fourteen**), as Edna waits for her husband to arrive from the hotel, she thinks about a song she and Robert sang as they crossed the bay: "The voice, the notes, the whole refrain haun[t] her memory."

In **chapter fifteen,** Edna is stunned to discover that Robert is leaving for Mexico. He insists, unconvincingly, that this has been his desire for many years. Edna concludes that she is suffering again from "the symptoms of infatuation which she had felt incipiently as a child . . . and later as a young woman." With Robert's departure, she is being "denied that which her impassioned, newly awakened being demanded." What "that" is seems as vague and as fantastic as Robert's fanciful stories.

With Robert gone and the summer at Grand Isle nearly over (**chapter sixteen**), Edna finds her "only real pleasurable moments" in swimming. In a heated conversation with a baffled Madame Ratignolle, she attempts to define her newly awakened sense of self: "I would give up the unessential; I would give my money, I would give my life for my children; but I wouldn't give myself. I can't make it more clear; it's only something which I am beginning to comprehend, which is revealing itself to me." This declaration will also mark the paradox of her ultimate awakening, her suicide.

In **chapter sixteen**, Mademoiselle Reisz emerges as one image of the life possible for a single woman of artistic sensibility at the turn of the twentieth century. She mirrors and distorts Edna's emerging vision of selfhood. Although she warms to Edna, she is a disagreeable and solitary figure. Her aversion to swimming symbolizes the way she is different in temperament from Edna. She is also a malicious gossip who nonetheless satisfies Edna's need to talk about Robert, no matter the subject.

In the six years that the Pontelliers have been married, Edna has "religiously followed" a social schedule centered in their "charming" and "conventional" home in New Orleans (**chapter seventeen**). Mr. Pontellier is "very fond of walking about his house examining its various appointments and details, to see that nothing was amiss. He greatly valued his possessions, chiefly because they were his." Edna is one of these possessions, and Léonce is unhappy with her household management; the dinner displeases him and, as has happened often before, he leaves for "the club." In the past, these familiar scenes caused her regret and a belated rebuke to the cook. This evening, however, Edna is enraged; she smashes a vase and throws her wedding ring to the floor, attempting to crush it under her heel. The alarmed maid enters and picks up the ring, which Edna slips back on her finger without comment.

The morning brings no change in her mood (**chapter eighteen**). Edna no longer has any interest in her home, her children, or her surroundings. They are "all part and parcel of an alien world which had suddenly become antagonistic." Edna gathers her best sketches to bring to Madame Ratignolle, still her most intimate friend. The beautiful and efficient Madame Ratignolle looks at Edna's drawings and proclaims that her "talent is immense." Although Edna knows that her friend's opinion is "next to valueless," she wants her praise and encouragement. Edna had hoped to find comfort and reassurance amidst the "domestic harmony" of the Ratignolle household but is instead depressed after she leaves. Unlike Adèle, Edna feels consumed by "life's delirium."

By **chapter nineteen**, Edna has abandoned both household management and emotional outbursts, "going and coming as it suited her fancy, and, so far as she was able, lending herself to any passing caprice." The sense of her growing independence, though, is tempered by the knowledge that a penalty will be exacted for this freedom. Léonce suspects that she might be "growing a little unbalanced mentally." Paradoxically, the less Edna seems to be "herself" in his eyes the more she is "becoming herself." Her mood alternates between happiness at simply being alive and depression, "when life appeared to her like a grotesque pandemonium and humanity like worms struggling blindly toward inevitable annihilation."

Later, Edna is determined to visit Mademoiselle Reisz, to hear her play the piano (**chapter twenty**). Edna must see Madame Lebrun to find Mademoiselle Reisz's address. Madame Lebrun shares Robert's letters from Vera Cruz and Mexico City, but Edna is "despondent" that she can detect no message to herself in them. She departs with Mademoiselle Reisz's address; Madame Lebrun and Victor remark to each other how beautiful Edna looks. In some way, Victor observes, "she doesn't seem like the same woman."

Mademoiselle Reisz lives in a small apartment crowded by a "magnificent piano" and little else. The "strikingly homely" musician is delighted to see Edna (**chapter twenty-one**), laughing with "a contortion of the face and all the muscles of the body." Edna is amazed when Mademoiselle Reisz reveals that she has received a letter from Robert that is "nothing but Mrs. Pontellier from beginning to end." Robert has told Mademoiselle Reisz to play for Edna his favorite piece, the Impromptu of Chopin (a small joke, most likely, on the author's part).

Léonce Pontellier consults the family physician, Doctor Mandelet, about Edna (**chapter twenty-two**). "She's got some sort of notion in her head concerning the eternal rights of women; and—you understand—we meet in the morning at the breakfast table." Until this point in the story, Edna's struggle has been internal, psychological. In this chapter, Chopin attempts to supply a more obvious social and political frame for Edna's distress. The doctor responds accordingly, "[H]as she been associating of late with a circle of pseudo-intellectual women—super-spiritual superior beings? My wife has been telling me about them." Edna's altered perceptions cannot be so easily diagnosed, however. She associates with no one. "[S]he goes tramping about by herself . . . getting in after dark," Léonce replies, "I tell you she's peculiar. I don't like it." The doctor advises him to leave Edna alone, that this may be just "some passing whim." A woman, he adds, is "a very peculiar and delicate organism." The doctor privately suspects that another man may be the source of Edna's behavior.

Edna's father, the Colonel, comes to New Orleans to buy a wedding gift for his other daughter, Janet, in **chapter twenty-three**. Edna and her father are not close, although they have "certain tastes in common." Edna sketches him. He takes her efforts most seriously, convinced that all his daughters have inherited from him "the germs of a masterful capability." It is his only charm. They attend a "*soirée musicale*" at Madame Ratignolle's where Mademoiselle Reisz plays. The little musician and the Colonel flirt, and Edna, herself "almost devoid of coquetry," marvels at the spectacle.

Doctor Mandelet dines with the Pontelliers a few days later. He observes Edna's behavior for signs of some secret she may be suppressing. Instead, he finds that there is "no repression in her glance or gesture." She reminds him instead of "some beautiful, sleek animal waking up in the sun." As part of the evening's entertainment, Edna tells a story about a woman who leaves in a small boat with her lover one night, never to return. She falsely claims that Madame Antoine had related it to her: "Perhaps it was a dream she had had. But every glowing word seemed real to those who listened," including the doctor. As he leaves the Pontellier household, he regrets possessing the insight he has into the inner lives of others; he is weary of it. Chopin suggests that a practiced insight may be best left to women novelists such as she.

Edna and her father have an "almost violent" argument when she refuses to attend her sister Janet's wedding (**chapter twenty-four**). Her reasons are not revealed. Is Edna simply protesting the marriage? Following Doctor Mandelet's advice to allow Edna to do as she likes, Léonce refuses to intervene. The Colonel advises Léonce that he is too lenient with Edna. "Authority, coercion are what is needed. Put your foot down good and hard; the only way to manage a wife."

As if in imitation of Madame Ratignolle's domestic solicitude, Edna affectionately bids Léonce good-bye as he departs for

New York on business. His mother takes the children to her home at Iberville, fearing that Edna might neglect them. Edna fully enjoys the "radiant peace" of her solitude. She assumes an easy authority over the servants, enjoys her dinner, thinks briefly and sentimentally about Léonce and the children, reads Emerson until she grows sleepy, and retires with "a sense of restfulness . . . such as she had not known before."

In **chapter twenty-five**, Alcée Arobin emerges as "a familiar figure at the race course, the opera, the fashionable clubs." Charming, with a quiet though sometimes "insolent" manner, he is a frequent dinner companion for Edna. Arobin escorts Edna home on one such evening. She is restless, wanting "something to happen—something, anything; she did not know what." She regrets not having asked Arobin to stay and talk with her as she retires to a fretful sleep. A few days later, Arobin calls on Edna and the two spend the afternoon at the races. Edna enjoys Arobin's easy manner and frank conversation. He shows her a dueling scar on his wrist. Edna impulsively clutches his hand as she examines the "red cicatrice," then draws away suddenly, sickened by it. The incident, with its sudden intimacy, "drew all [Edna's] awakening sensuousness." In response, Arobin feels impelled "to take her hand and hold it while he said his lingering good night." Edna is not unaware of the seductive nature of this encounter, and she refuses to see Arobin again, though he insists that she allow him to return. Although Arobin is "absolutely nothing to her," the incident affects her "like a narcotic," and she retires to a "languorous sleep, interwoven with vanishing dreams."

The drama of the incident with Arobin embarrasses Edna in the "cooler, quieter moment[s]" of the following day (**chapter twenty-six**). Arobin sends a note of apology and comes to her home with "disarming naïveté." He adopts an attitude of "good-humored subservience and tacit adoration" in order to remain in her presence. Despite her initial embarrassment, the candor of his speech appeals to "the animalism that stirred impatiently within her."

Edna visits Mademoiselle Reisz (**chapter twenty-six**) and announces that she intends to move out of her house into "a little four-room house around the corner. . . . I'm tired," she explains, "looking after that big house. It never seemed like mine, anyway—like home." Mademoiselle Reisz shrewdly discerns that Robert Lebrun is the cause of Edna's "caprice." She reveals to Edna that Robert is coming back to New Orleans. To complicate matters, and to put Edna's emotions into even greater turmoil, Arobin kisses her the next evening **(chapter twenty-seven)**, "the first kiss of her life to which her nature had really responded. It was a flaming torch that kindled desire." That night **(chapter twenty-eight)** she has an "overwhelming feeling of irresponsibility," disturbed that she experiences "neither shame nor remorse" over a kiss that did not signify love, but lust.

Edna feverishly prepares to move into the little house **(chapter twenty-nine)**, without waiting for a response to the letter she has sent her husband. Edna moves "everything which she had acquired aside from her husband's bounty" into the new house, "supplying simple and meager deficiencies" from the small allowance she receives from her mother's estate. Arobin visits her, perplexed and alarmed by her activities, but impressed at her "splendid and robust" appearance as she works alongside her housemaid. She assures Arobin that she will still give the dinner she has planned for two days hence. She tells him it will have "my best of everything" and wonders what Léonce will say when he pays the bills; Arobin wryly titles the event Edna's *"coup d'état."*

Edna's dinner party, on her twenty-ninth birthday, is a "small affair and very select" **(chapter thirty)**. Among the guests are Arobin, Victor Lebrun, Mademoiselle Reisz, and Monsieur Ratignolle, Madame Lebrun and Adèle Ratignolle having characteristically sent their regrets. The table is "extremely gorgeous," and she wears a "cluster of diamonds that sparkled, that almost sputtered, in [her] hair," a present from her husband in New York. "[G]ood fellowship passed around [Edna and] the circle [of guests] like a mystic cord, holding and binding these people together with jest and laughter," until Victor, at the urging of the others, sings the song that Robert had sung to Edna on the boat that night. Edna cries out that he must stop, shattering her wine glass "blindly upon the table." He does not take her protests seriously, however, until she moves behind him and covers his mouth with her hand. He kisses her hand and becomes quiet; Edna finds that the "touch of his lips was like a pleasing sting to her hand." In response to this intense display, the other guests "suddenly conceived the notion that it was time to say good night."

Arobin remains after the other guests depart (**chapter thirty-one**). He walks her home from the cottage, nicknamed "the pigeon-house." She is cold, miserable, and tired, as if "she had been wound up to a certain pitch—too tight—and something inside . . . had snapped." Arobin gently smoothes her hair, and "[h]is touch conveyed to her a certain physical comfort. She could have fallen quietly asleep there if he had continued to pass his hand over her hair." He leaves only after Edna had become "supple to his gentle, seductive entreaties."

Stern correspondence from Mr. Pontellier, still in New York, expresses his "unqualified disapproval" of Edna's resolve to abandon her home (**chapter thirty-two**). To circumvent scandal, he announces in the "daily papers . . . that their handsome residence on Esplanade Street was undergoing sumptuous alterations, and would not be ready for occupancy until their return [from a trip abroad]." Edna is impressed with his resourcefulness in the matter of public opinion. She is more pleased with the "intimate character" of her new home. After a brief visit to her children, she is happy to return to the city to be "again alone."

Edna meets Madame Ratignolle at Mademoiselle Reisz's apartment (**chapter thirty-three**) and learns that gossip has linked her romantically to Alcée Arobin. "Does he boast of his successes?" Edna asks, affecting disinterest. After Adèle departs, Mrs. Merriman and Mrs. Highcamp, named as if characters in a Restoration comedy, arrive and ask Edna to attend dinner and a game of "*vingt-et-un*" (twenty-one). Arobin has agreed to escort her home afterward, they tell her, and Edna accepts in a "half-hearted way."

Edna waits for Mademoiselle Reisz to arrive. She is stunned when Robert Lebrun appears at the door. They exchange small talk, and Edna mistakenly believes that his feelings for her have changed. She decides to return home, and Robert, "as if suddenly aware of some discourtesy in his speech," offers to escort her. She asks him what he has been "seeing and doing and feeling out there in Mexico." He confesses being preoccupied with "the waves and white beach of Grand Isle," he tells her, "the quiet, grassy street of the *Chênière*; the old fort at Grande Terre . . . and feeling like a lost soul." He asks her the same question she has asked him, to which she gives the same reply; she, too, feels like "a lost soul."

Edna and Robert dine together at the pigeon-house in **chapter thirty-four**. Their conversation becomes formal, with "no return to personalities." Afterward, once more alone, Edna is perplexed because he had "seemed nearer to her off there in Mexico" than he does in New Orleans. When she wakes the next morning (**chapter thirty-five**), Edna is certain that Robert loves her, and she regrets her "despondency" of the previous evening. She paints "with much spirit" for several hours, hoping that Robert will return; but three days later he has not. One night she goes riding with Arobin and they return to the little house to dine. His "delicate sense of her nature's requirements like a torpid, torrid, sensitive blossom" evokes a response in Edna. Although she awakes the next morning without "despondency," she has lost all sense of "hope."

Chapter thirty-six opens in a garden in the suburbs of New Orleans. The garden, like Edna and her pigeon-house, is a "place too modest to attract the attention of people of fashion, and so quiet as to have escaped the notice of those in search of pleasure and dissipation." Edna's life and story are that of an ordinary woman. Later in the evening, Robert arrives unexpectedly. He admits that he left for Mexico to avoid her; he has been "fighting" his feelings for her since last summer at Grand Isle. Edna tells him that he had awakened her "out of a life-long, stupid dream." To add complication, Madame Ratignolle sends word that she is ill and asks Edna to come immediately. Robert begs Edna to stay there with him. She promises to return: "I shall come back as soon as I can; I shall find you here." The bedridden Adèle concludes **chapter thirty-seven** with a melodramatic plea to Edna that she "think of the children!"

Doctor Mandelet, aware of Edna's distress over Madame Ratignolle's remark, walks Edna home (**chapter thirty-eight**): "You shouldn't have been there, Mrs. Pontellier," he said, "That was no place for you. Adèle is full of whims at such times. There were a dozen women she might have had with her, unimpressionable women. I felt that it was cruel, cruel. You shouldn't have gone." "I don't know that it matters after all," she responds. "One has to think of the children some time or other; the sooner the better." Doctor Mandelet is, apparently, a practitioner of the then new psychological precepts that would shape Freudian therapy. He urges Edna to consult with him at his office to "talk of things you never have dreamt of talking about before." Robert does not wait for Edna to return, but he leaves a note: "I love you. Good-by—because I love you." She remains awake all night.

In the final chapter of *The Awakening*, Edna returns alone to Grand Isle, which is deserted until summer. Victor, making repairs, is describing to Mariequita the sumptuous dinner he attended at the Pontelliers, when both are stunned to see Mrs. Pontellier walking toward them from the dock. He offers her his room, since there is "nothing fixed up yet." Edna tells them that she has come to rest and to swim in the cold gulf. In response to protests that the water is "too cold" to swim, Edna assures them that she will only "dip [her] toes in" and sends Mariequita to find her some towels. Her movements are mechanical. She notices nothing except that the sun is hot as she walks down to the beach. She has nothing more to think about now that Robert has abandoned her. In a paragraph that may be the key to the scandal this tale provoked when it was published, Edna reflects: "To-day it is Arobin; to-morrow it will be some one else. It makes no difference to me, it doesn't matter about Léonce Pontellier—but Raoul and Etienne!" She understood now clearly what she had meant long ago when she said to Adèle Ratignolle that she would give up the unessential, but she would never sacrifice herself for her children." At the edge of the water, "absolutely alone," she takes off her clothes and, "for the first time in her life she stood naked in the open air . . . and the waves . . . invited her." As the water "enfold[s her] body in its soft, close embrace," she recalls her terror of being "unable to regain the shore" last summer, but now she thinks of a place she had known in childhood and which she thought "had no beginning and no end." Fatigue overwhelms her as she swims past the point of return, awakened to the magnitude of her unconscious self while simultaneously unable to bear it.

Critical Views

DOROTHY DIX ON UNSELFISHNESS

Women have been extolled for their unselfishness so long that it comes with a shock of surprise to learn that their pet virtue has at last been called into question. Nay, it has been more than questioned. It has been positively asserted that woman is the very quintessence of selfishness. It is boldly charged that she thinks of nothing but her own pleasures, amusements and interest. She is accused of belonging to clubs that are neither more nor less than mutual admiration societies, where women meet together to glorify their own sex and formulate plans for its advancement. Worse than that, she goes off in summer to the mountains or seaside, leaving her poor down-trodden husband to swelter in the city, without even the reward of a cool smile or a frozen glance when he returns home at night after his arduous day's work. If this is not ingrained, hopeless, conscienceless selfishness, the critics would just like to know what is, that's all.

From time immemorial it has been the custom of woman to sacrifice herself whenever she got a chance, and any deflection from the course she was expected to pursue must necessarily occasion a deal of comment. Unselfishness with her has been a cult. She has worn it ostentatiously, and flaunted it in the face of the world with a feeling that it would make good any other deficiencies or shortcomings. She has courted persecution, and gone out of her way to become a martyr. She has accounted it unto herself for righteousness to do those things she did not wish to do, and to leave undone those things she was dying to do. On the platform of pure and unadulterated unselfishness she has taken a stand, and defied competition, and now when she wishes to climb down and off, and give other people a chance to practice the virtue they admire so much, she is cruelly misjudged and assailed.

It must be admitted in all fairness that this attitude of perfect self-abnegation is one which men have never failed to praise, but seldom emulated. Men have always taken a saner view of life than women. A woman sacrifices herself in a thousand needless little ways which do no one any good, but when a man makes a sacrifice it is big with heroism, and counts. A woman thinks she is being good when she is uncomfortable. A man knows people are much more apt to be good when they are comfortable. No man with a full purse and a full stomach was ever an anarchist.

The truth of the matter simply is that women have awakened to the fact that they have been overdoing the self-sacrifice business. A reasonable amount of unselfishness is all right. It is the sense of justice with which we recognize other people's rights; it is the love that makes us prefer another to ourselves; it is the adorable grace and sweetness that softens a strong and independent character, and is as far different as possible from the lack of backbone that weakly gives away before everything and everybody.

—from *The Times Picayune*

"The Awakening" is the sad story of a Southern lady who wanted to do what she wanted to. From wanting to, she did, with disastrous consequences; but as she swims out to sea in the end, it is to be hoped that her example may lie for ever undredged. It is with high expectation that we open the volume, remembering the author's agreeable short stories, and with real disappointment that we close it. The recording reviewer drops a tear over one more clever author gone wrong. Mrs. Chopin's accustomed fine workmanship is here, the hinted effects, the well expended epithet, the pellucid style; and, so far as construction goes, the writer shows herself as competent to write a novel as a sketch. The tint and air of Creole New Orleans and the Louisiana seacoast are conveyed to the reader with subtle skill, and among the secondary characters are several that are lifelike. But we cannot see that literature or the criticism of life is helped by the detailed history of the manifold and contemporary love affairs of a wife and mother. Had she lived by Prof. William James's[1] advice to do one thing a day one does not want to do (in Creole society, two would perhaps be better), flirted less and looked after her children more, or even assisted at more *accouchements*—her *chef d'oeuvre* in self-denial—we need not have been put to the unpleasantness of reading about her and the temptations she trumped up for herself.

Note

1. American philosopher (1842–1910), known as a "radical pragmatist," author of influential books on religion and psychology, and brother of the novelist Henry James.

—from *The Nation*

PERCIVAL POLLARD QUESTIONS THE SERIOUSNESS OF EDNA'S PASSION

This seemed a subject for the physician, not the novelist. So skilfully and so hardily does the book reveal the growth of animalism in a woman, that we feel as if we were attending a medical lecture. In the old days—when men, mere men such as Balzac or Flaubert or Gautier, attempted this sort of dissection—we were wont to sigh, and think what brutes they must be to suppose women made of this poor clay. Surely it was only the males who harbored thoughts fit only for the smoking-room; surely—but, Pouff! Kate Chopin dispelled those dreams.

"The Awakening" asked us to believe that a young woman who had been several years married, and had borne children, had never, in all that time, been properly "awake." It would be an arresting question for students of sleep-walking; but one must not venture down that bypath now. Her name was *Edna Pontellier*. She was married to a man who had Creole blood in him; yet the marrying, and the having children, and all the rest of it, had left her still slumbrous, still as innocent of her physical self, as the young girl who graduates in the early summer would have us believe she is. She was almost at the age that Balzac held so dangerous—almost she was the Woman of Thirty—yet she had not properly tasted the apple of knowledge. She had to wait until she met a young man who was not her husband, was destined to tarry until she was under the influence of a Southern moonlight and the whispers of the Gulf and many other passionate things, before there began in her the first faint flushings of desire. So, at any rate, Kate Chopin asked us to believe.

The cynic was forced to observe that simply because a young woman showed interest in a man who was not her husband, especially at a fashionable watering-place, in a month when the blood was hottest, there was no need to argue the aforesaid fair female had lain coldly dormant all her life. There are women in the world quite as versatile as the butterfly, and a sprouting of the physical today need not mean that yesterday was all spiritual.

However, taking Kate Chopin's word for it that Edna had been asleep, her awakening was a most champagne-like performance. After she met *Robert Lebrun* the awakening stirred in her, to use a rough simile, after the manner of ferment in new wine. *Robert* would, I fancy, at any Northern summer resort have been sure of a lynching; for, after a trifling encounter with him, Edna became utterly unmanageable. She neglected her house; she tried to paint—always a bad sign, that, when women want to paint, or act, or sing, or write!—and the while she painted there was "a subtle current of desire passing through her body, weakening her hold upon the brushes and making her eyes burn."

Does that not explain to you certain pictures you have seen? Now you know how the artist came to paint them just like that.

To think of Kate Chopin, who once contented herself with mild yarns about genteel Creole life—pages almost clean enough to put into the Sunday school library—blowing us a hot blast like that! Well, San Francisco, and Paris, and London, and New York had furnished Women Who Did; why not New Orleans?

"The black line of his leg moving in and out. . . ." Why, even that Japo-German apostle of plaquet-prose, Sadakichi Hartmann, did not surpass this when he wrote in his "Lady of the Yellow Jonquils": "She drew her leg, that was nearest to me, with a weavy graceful motion to her body. . . ."

It may seem indelicate, in view of where we left *Edna*, to return to her at once; we must let some little time elapse. Imagine, then, the time elapsed, and *Robert* returned. He did not know that *Arobin* had been taking a hand in *Edna's* awakening. *Robert* had gone away, it seems, because he scrupled to love *Edna*, she being married. But *Edna* had no scruples left; she hastened to intimate to *Robert* that she loved him, that her husband meant nothing to her. Never, by any chance, did she mention *Arobin*. But dear me, *Arobin*, to a woman like that, had been merely an incident; he merely happened to hold the torch. Now, what in the world do you suppose that *Robert* did? Went away—pouff!—like that! Went away, saying he loved *Edna* too well to—well, to partake of the fire the other youth had lit. Think of it! *Edna* finally awake—completely, fiercely awake—and the man she had waked up for goes away!

Of course, she went and drowned herself. She realised that you can only put out fire with water, if all other chemical engines go away. She realised that the awakening was too great, that she was too aflame; that it was now merely Man, not Robert or Arobin, that she desired. So she took an infinite dip in the passionate Gulf.

Cyrille Arnavon on the Worthiness of *The Awakening*

Although Kate Chopin's applied symbolism depends on an aestheticism that does not really impress us, one remains, nevertheless, convinced that this portrayal of a woman is on the whole correct. We are, of course, aware that in Kate Chopin's psychology and dramatic art there are some weaknesses that leave us somewhat confused. To her translator, Edna's story seems firmly anchored in a common experience shared by all those who have made a careful study of real life—an experience providing material for any solid piece of work, whether it be a poem, play, or novel. *The Awakening* is something more than a mere curiosity in American literature, and it is something more than just a welcome novel about a woman. Yet for some unknown reason, it never found its way into the library catalogues and contemporary manuals written for the benefit of later generations.

This tragic novel goes far beyond the conscious intentions of Kate Chopin, who originally meant to describe the dullness of the life of a bourgeoise who, for our convenience, she placed in New Orleans. We have already used the word *symbolism*; but a clear symbolism, a completely intellectual reconstruction, remains on the level of a witticism or intellectual game. Without, however, making our interpretation too limited by using a too systematic terminology that Kate Chopin could not possibly have known, we can easily see a kind of regressive fixation in Edna Pontellier and, through her, in her creator. The presence of a youthful and fairly attractive father is possibly the root of this psychosis. The attraction to the sea, which from her early childhood has been represented by the blue fields of Kentucky (significant because there do not seem to be any large expanses of water where Edna grew up), corresponds to a longing (often the result of a trauma) to return to the mother's womb.

Likewise, Edna's inexplicable suicide, which seems to stem from her negative attitude toward life, is in reality a flight from sexual experience. The reader will remember that Edna, with her strict Puritan upbringing and resulting repressions and inhibitions, once confided in Adèle Ratignolle. Since early adolescence, her gestures and descriptions of herself reveal, she possessed a very ardent temperament. She had felt attracted to men who for some reason or other were inaccessible: the cavalry officer, the engaged man, the actor. Subsequently, she displays an affection for her brilliant and headstrong fellow vacationer Adèle Ratignolle which neither she herself nor Kate Chopin was able to explain. She let herself be married, primarily as a reaction against her own family and the atmosphere prevailing in her home.

The writer leaves no doubt that Edna's marriage to Pontellier was never satisfying. Indeed, her attitude towards her two sons can be said to be that of a discontented woman. After a few years, she is no longer her husband's wife except in name; and with Arobin, she experiences a second failure because she can not help thinking about Robert. Arobin, detached at first, becomes more and more enthralled by Edna's physical attraction. The explanation for Edna's failure may be that complex characters like her can he attracted by only a very limited number of people, as was convincingly demonstrated by Dr. Marañon with regard to Amiel.[5]

As for Robert Lebrun, the existence of social taboos against a relationship which is the only kind that would have satisfied Edna, causes the relationship to end because of outside pressures. And the attraction the water holds for her, symbolizing a return to a pre-natal existence, becomes gradually stronger. Something similar had happened during her vacation in Grand Isle, a period in which she felt more dissatisfied than usual. One is left with a feeling that if she had not refused Arobin for Robert's sake—in itself a logical consequence of Arobin's erotic behavior—and if Robert had not most inopportunely vanished, Edna would in time have surmounted her psychological difficulties. Might not her trusted physician, Mandelet, better at curing souls than healing bodies, have succeeded in exorcising the evil spirits that were haunting her? Perhaps he would. Indeed, at the very moment when she throws herself into the water (end of Chapter XXXIX), Edna has not yet altogether given up hope. But this hope of recovery, which would probably have proved illusory if she had only consulted the old family doctor and no one else, would very likely have been fulfilled if she had been able to consult Dr. Freud.[6]

It is strange and at the same time suggestive that the general construction of the book and, even more, certain seemingly insignificant details like the attraction exercised by the water, integral to Edna's fictional personality, should seem, even to an ordinary reader, to accord very well with a number of observations and interpretations which are now common knowledge. If a psychoanalyst were to read this text carefully, he might perhaps be able to see what is autobiographical and what is not.

But this brief account, restricted to a few selected hypotheses, may perhaps suffice to convince a literary critic or even an ordinary reader that there is something worth remembering in Edna Pontellier's pathetic story. One may have read ten or twenty novels of this type without retaining anything except a very blurred outline of the various plots, because the whole presentation was too stylized. On the other hand, greater and weightier works like those modelled upon Flaubert's novel, such as the story told by Kate Chopin, a lucid and sensitive woman who seems very close to us today, although she lived nearly a hundred years ago—that story, though heavily influenced by aestheticism, could assume a permanent value both as a warning and as a confession.

Notes
5. See Gregario Marañon, *Amiel: on estudio sobre la timidez* (Madrid: Espasa-Calpe, 1932). The book is a study of Henri-Frederic Amiel's *Fragments d'un journal intime* (Paris, 1883–87, 1923, 1927).
6. Sigmund Freud (1856–1939), Austrian founder of modern psychoanalysis.

KENNETH EBLE ON CHOPIN'S VIRTUES AS A WRITER

Here is the story, its beginning a mature woman's awakening to physical love, its end her walking into the sea. The extracts convey something of the author's style, but much less of the movement of the characters and of human desire against the sensuous background of sea and sand. Looking at the novel analytically, one can say that it excels chiefly in its characterizations and its structure, the use of images and symbols to unify that structure, and the character of Edna Pontellier.

Kate Chopin, almost from her first story, had the ability to capture character, to put the right word in the mouth, to impart the exact gesture, to select the characteristic action. An illustration of her deftness in handling even minor characters is her treatment of Edna's father. When he leaves the Pontelliers' after a short visit, Edna is glad to be rid of him and "his padded shoulders, his Bible reading, his 'toddies,' and ponderous oaths." A moment later, it is a side of Edna's nature which is revealed. She felt a sense of relief at her father's absence; "she read Emerson until she grew sleepy."

Characterization was always Mrs. Chopin's talent. Structure was not. Those who knew her working habits say that she seldom revised, and she herself mentions that she did not like reworking her stories. Though her reputation rests upon her short narratives, her collected stories give abundant evidence of the sketch, the outlines of stories which remain unformed. And when she did attempt a tightly organized story, she often turned to Maupassant and was as likely as not to effect a contrived symmetry. Her early novel *At Fault* suffers most from her inability to control her material. In *The Awakening* she is in complete command of structure. She seems to have grasped instinctively the use of the unifying symbol—here the sea, sky and sand—and with it the power of individual images to bind the story together.

The sea, the sand, the sun and sky of the Gulf Coast become almost a presence themselves in the novel. Much of the sensuousness of the book comes from the way the reader is never allowed to stray far from the water's edge. A refrain beginning "The voice of the sea is seductive, never ceasing, clamoring, murmuring, . . ." is used throughout the novel. It appears first at the beginning of Edna Pontellier's awakening, and it appears at the end as the introduction to the long final scene, previously quoted. Looking closely at the final form of this refrain, one can notice the care with which Mrs. Chopin composed this theme and variation. In the initial statement, the sentence does not end with "solitude," but goes on, as it should, "to lose itself in mazes of inward contemplation." Nor is the image of the bird with the broken wing in the earlier passage; rather there is a prefiguring of the final tragedy: "The voice of the sea speaks to the soul. The touch of the sea is sensuous, enfolding the body in its soft close embrace." The way scene, mood, action and character are fused reminds one not so much of literature as of an impressionist painting, of a Renoir with much of the sweetness missing. Only Stephen Crane, among her American contemporaries, had an equal sensitivity to light and shadow, color and texture, had the painter's eye matched with the writer's perception of character and incident.

The best example of Mrs. Chopin's use of a visual image which is also highly symbolic is the lady in black and the two nameless lovers. They are seen as touches of paint upon the canvas and as indistinct yet evocative figures which accompany Mrs. Pontellier and Robert Lebrun during the course of their intimacy. They appear first early in the novel. "The lady in black was reading her morning devotions on the porch of a neighboring bath house. Two young lovers were exchanging their heart's yearning beneath the children's tent which they had found unoccupied." Throughout the course of Edna's awakening, these figures appear and reappear, the lovers entering the pension, leaning toward each other as the water-oaks bent from the sea, the lady in black, creeping behind them. They accompany Edna and Robert when they first go to the Chênière, "the lovers, shoulder to shoulder, creeping, the lady in black, gaining steadily upon them." When Robert departs for Mexico, the picture changes. Lady and lovers depart together, and Edna finds herself back from the sea and shore, and set among her human acquaintances, her husband; her father; Mme. [sic] Reisz, the musician, "a homely woman with a small wizened face and body, and eyes that glowed"; Alcée Arobin; Mme. Ratignolle; and others. One brief scene from this milieu will further illustrate Mrs. Chopin's conscious or unconscious symbolism.

The climax of Edna's relationship with Arobin is the dinner which is to celebrate her last night in her and her husband's house. Edna is ready to move to a small place around the corner where she can escape (though she does not phrase it this way) the feeling that she is one more of Léonce Pontellier's possessions. At the dinner Victor Lebrun, Robert's brother, begins singing, "Ah! si tu savais!" a song which brings back all her memories of Robert. She sets her glass so blindly down that she shatters it against the carafe. "The wine spilled over Arobin's legs and some of it trickled down upon Mrs. Highcamp's black gauze gown." After the other guests have gone, Edna and Arobin walk to the new house. Mrs. Chopin writes of Edna, "She looked down, noticing the black line of his leg moving in and out so close to her against the yellow shimmer of her gown." The chapter concludes:

His hand had strayed to her beautiful shoulders, and he could feel the response of her flesh to his touch. He seated himself beside her and kissed her lightly upon the shoulder.

"I thought you were going away," she said, in an uneven voice.

"I am, after I have said good night."

"Good night," she murmured.

He did not answer, except to continue to caress her. He did not say good night until she had become supple to his gentle, seductive entreaties.

It is not surprising that the sensuous quality of the book, both from the incidents of the novel and the symbolic implications, would have offended contemporary reviewers. What convinced many critics of the indecency of the book, however, was not simply the sensuous scenes, but rather that the author obviously sympathized with Mrs. Pontellier. More than that, the readers probably found that she aroused their own sympathies.

STANLEY KAUFFMANN PRAISES *THE AWAKENING* FOR ITS ORIGINALITY

Like Emma Bovary, Edna Pontellier is an attractive young woman married to a well-meaning dullard, she is a mother, she is involved with two men, she commits suicide. Mrs. Chopin is not Flaubert's equal; her book does not have Flaubert's complexity of character or subtlety of orchestration; it lacks the breadth of context to make its intense anguish seem like an ironic winking moment in cosmic nonchalance; and there is no one scene in *The Awakening* that is conceived with the genius of such an episode as the one between Emma and Rodolphe at the agricultural fair. But there are two respects in which Mrs.

Chopin's novel is *harder* than Flaubert's, more ruthless, more insistent on truth of inner and social life as sole motivation. Edna Pontellier has her first affair out of sexual hunger, without romantic furbelow. She is in love, but the young man she loves has left New Orleans (where most of the novel takes place). Increasingly aware that her life is increasingly empty, she has a sheerly sexual affair with an accomplished amorist. And, second, Mrs. Chopin uses no equivalent of the complicated financial maneuvers with which Flaubert finally corners his heroine. Edna kills herself solely because of the foredoomed emptiness of a life stretching ahead of her. It is purely a psychological motive, untouched by plot contrivance.

The patent theme is in its title (a remarkably simple one for its day): the awakening of a conventional young woman to what is missing in her marriage, and her refusal to be content. Below that theme is the still-pertinent theme of the disparity between woman's sexual being and the rules of marriage. And below *that* is the perennial theme of nature versus civilization. The atmosphere of the book is that of frilled and formal New Orleans society (for, unlike Emma, Edna is not a provincial); but the book begins and ends with the sea.

It opens on Grand Isle in the Gulf of Mexico where the Pontelliers are summering, and it closes there. The very same sentence, about "the voice of the sea," occurs twice in the book. The first time, early in the story, is shortly after the following passage:

> Mrs. Pontellier was beginning to realize her position in the universe as a human being, and to recognize her relations as an individual to the world within and about her ... perhaps more wisdom than the Holy Ghost is usually pleased to vouchsafe to any woman.

The sentence about the sea occurs once more, near the very end, just after the following:

> Despondency had come upon her there in the wakeful night, and had never lifted. There was no one thing

in the world that she desired. There was no human being whom she wanted near her except Robert [the young man she loves]; and she even realized that the day would come when he, too, and the thought of him would melt out of her existence, leaving her alone. The children appeared before her like antagonists who had overpowered and sought to drag her into the soul's slavery for the rest of her days. But she knew a way to elude them. She was not thinking of these things when she walked down to the beach.

I submit that this is an extraordinary paragraph for an American novel published in 1899. It is neither Nora Helmer nor Susan B. Anthony. It is an anachronistic, lonely, existentialist voice out of the mid-20th century.

In the post-Freudian age, a certain patronizing view creeps into our reading of novels like this one, as if we thought that the author did very well considering that he didn't know as much about these matters as we do. An accompanying aspect is that we tend to give credit, even to Flaubert, on extra-literary grounds—pats on the head for being a pioneer. Still, after those aspects are either discounted or reckoned on, *The Awakening* remains a novel of high quality, fine in itself and astonishing for its day.

CYNTHIA GRIFFIN WOLFF ON THE PSYCHOLOGICAL ASPECTS OF EDNA'S LIFE

Given the apparent terror which genuine emotional involvement inspires in Edna, her marriage to a man like Léonce Pontellier is no accident. No one would call him remarkable; most readers might think him dull, insensitive, unperceptive, even callous. Certainly he is an essentially prosaic man. If one assumed that marriage was to be an intimate affair of deep understanding, all of these qualities would condemn Léonce. Yet for Edna they are the very qualities which recommend him. "The acme of bliss, which would have been a marriage with the tragedian, was not for her in this world"; such bliss, indeed, is not for anyone *in this world*. It is a romantic allusion, a dream—defined by its very inability to be consummated. What is more, the intensity of dreams such as these may have become disturbing to Edna. So she chooses to marry Léonce; after all "as the devoted wife of a man who worshiped her, she felt she would take her place with a certain dignity in the world of reality, closing the portals forever behind her upon the realm of romance and dreams." The marriage to such a man as Léonce was, then, a defensive maneuver designed to maintain the integrity of the two "selves" that formed her character and to reinforce the distance between them. Her outer self was confirmed by the entirely conventional marriage while her inner self was safe—known only to Edna. An intuitive man, a sensitive husband, might threaten it; a husband who evoked passion from her might lure the hidden self into the open, tempting Edna to attach her emotions to flesh and blood rather than phantoms. Léonce is neither, and their union ensures the secret safety of Edna's "real" self.

If we try to assess the configuration of Edna's personality when she comes to Grand Isle at the novel's beginning, we might best do so by using R. D. Laing's description of the "schizoid" personality. As Laing would describe it, the schizoid personality consists of a set of defenses which have been established as an attempt to preserve some semblance of coherent identity. "The self, in order to develop and sustain its identity and autonomy, and in order to be safe from the persistent threat and danger from the world, has cut itself off from direct relatedness with others, and has endeavoured to become its own object: to become, in fact, related directly only to itself. Its cardinal functions become phantasy and observation. Now, in so far as this is successful, one necessary consequence is that the self has difficulty sustaining any *sentiment du réel* for the very reason that it is not 'in touch' with reality, it never actually 'meets' reality."

Laing's insights provide at least a partial explanation for elements of the novel which might otherwise be unclear. For example, Edna's fragility or susceptibility to the atmosphere at

Grand Isle (as compared, for example, with her robust friend Madame Ratignolle, or the grand aloofness of Madame Reisz) can be traced to the circular ineffectiveness of the schizoid mechanism for maintaining identity. To be specific, such a person must be simultaneously alert to and protected from any invitation to interact with the real world since all genuine interactions leave the hidden "real" self exposed to potential danger. Vigilance begets threat which in turn precipitates withdrawal and renewed vigilance.

More important, interpersonal relationships can be conceived of only in cataclysmic terms; "there is a constant dread and resentment at being turned into someone else's thing, of being penetrated by him, and a sense of being in someone else's power and control. Freedom then consists in being inaccessible." Such habits of mind comport with Edna's outbursts concerning her own relationships. Certainly her rather dull husband seems not to notice her except as part of the general inventory of his worldly goods: thus early in the novel he is described as "looking at his wife as one looks at a valuable piece of personal property which has suffered some damage." Yet his attentions, such as they are, are rather more indicative of indifference than otherwise. Indeed, at every point within the narrative when he might, were he so inclined, assert his "rights," he declines to do so. After the evening swimming party, for example, when he clearly desires sexual intercourse and his wife does not wish to comply, he utters but a few sharp words and then, surprising for a man so supposedly interested in the proprietary relationship, slips on a robe and comes out to keep her company during her fitful vigil. After the return to New Orleans, he reacts to Edna's disruption of her "wifely functions" with but momentary impatience; he does not attempt coercion, and he goes to the lengths of consulting a physician out of concern for her well-being. Even when Edna has taken up residence in her diminutive "pigeon-house" Léonce decides to leave her to her own ways. His only concern—a small-minded one, to be sure—is to save appearances.

It is hard to cast such an ultimately insignificant man in the role of villain. Léonce is a slender vehicle to carry the weight of society's repression of women. Yet Edna sees herself as his possession, even as she sees herself the prisoner of her children's demands. Her dying thoughts confirm this fixation: "She thought of Léonce and the children. They were a part of her life. But they need not have thought that they could possess her, body and soul." Now if Léonce is not able to rise to the occasion of possessing her body and soul, the children as they are portrayed in the novel, seem to exercise even less continuous claim upon her. They are always accompanied by a nurse whose presence frees Edna to pursue whatever interests she can sustain; what is more, they spend much of their time with their paternal grandmother, who seems to welcome them whenever Edna wishes to send them. Her emotional relationship with them is tenuous at best, certainly not demanding and by no stretch of the imagination stifling. "She was fond of her children in an uneven, impulsive way. She would sometimes gather them passionately to her heart; she would sometimes forget them." Given the extraordinary latitude that Edna did in fact have, we might better interpret her feelings of imprisonment as projections of her own attitudes and fears. The end of the novel offers an ironic affirmation of such a view, for when she returns home from Madame Ratignolle's accouchement, even her apparently positive expectations with regard to Robert follow the same familiar definition: "She could picture at that moment no greater bliss on earth than possession of the beloved one." The wording is somewhat ambiguous—she might possess him, he might possess her, the "possession" might be understood as a synonym for sexual union—still the key word here is *possession*, and it is Edna's word.

LAWRENCE THORNTON ON EDNA'S INEVITABLE FAILURE

For roughly the first half of the novel Chopin subordinates the political implications of Edna's predicament to the solitude and tentative self-exploration that begins to occupy her heroine during the summer idyll on Grand Isle. In the opening scenes Edna's undefined sense of longing is symbolized by the voice of the sea, which encourages the soul "to lose itself in mazes of inward contemplation," so that the relationships between Edna's isolation, her romantic sensibility, and the social significance of her situation do not emerge with any clarity until the guests at Madame Lebrun's establishment gather for an evening of entertainment. Even then, there is no specific statement to link the motifs together; what Chopin gives us instead is the motif of music, which indirectly leads to images of flight and escape. As Mademoiselle Reisz begins to play the piano, Edna recalls the pleasure she derives from listening to her friend, Adèle, when she practices. One piece Adèle plays Edna calls "Solitude": "When she heard it there came before her imagination the figure of a man standing beside a desolate rock on the seashore. He was naked. His attitude was one of hopeless resignation as he looked toward a distant bird winging its flight away from him" (pp. 26–27). The image of the bird does not assume its full significance as a unifying symbol for another sixty pages when Edna remembers a comment of Mademoiselle Reisz's as she and Alcée sit before the fire in the "pigeon house": "when I left today," she tells him, "she put her arms around me and felt my shoulder blades to see if my wings were strong, she said. 'The bird that would soar above the level plain of tradition and prejudice must have strong wings. It is a sad spectacle to see the weaklings bruised, exhausted, fluttering back to earth'" (p. 82). As the reader knows, escape from the Labyrinth of self or tradition demands a cunning Edna does not possess. This failure is made explicit on the final page of the novel when she returns to *Chênière Caminada*: "A bird with a broken wing was beating the air above, reeling, fluttering, circling disabled down, down to the water" (p. 113). Trapped in romantic longings whose objects are always vague and shifting in her mind's eye, and in a culture whose codes of duty and responsibility make escape impossible for even the most reluctant of "mother-women" (p. 10), Edna's fate is clearly foreshadowed in the imagery of defeated flight Chopin weaves into *The Awakening*.

At this point, we need to ask why, in a novel addressing woman's fate in society, Chopin chose a male figure to symbolize her heroine's solitude. The reason stems from Chopin's having realized that, on an unconscious level, Edna can only imagine a man in a position suggesting freedom and escape. His failure represents Edna's projection of herself onto the imagined figure. This view is consonant with the rest of the novel where we see that only men are free to act as they like and to go where they want: Robert to Mexico, Léonce to New York, Alcée from bed to bed. Whether it is Grand Isle, *Chênière Caminada*, or New Orleans, men escape, women remain. The New Woman Edna feels emerging from her "fictitious self" (p. 57) demands the prerogatives of men, but in making these demands she can only be destroyed by over-reaching in society that has no place for her.

But there are other reasons beyond the fact that there was little hope for independent women in New Orleans at the turn of the century that must be considered in an account of Edna's failure. Simply put, she cannot see beyond the romantic prison of imagination. To illustrate her myopia, Chopin introduces Mademoiselle Reisz, whose clarity of mind offers a striking contrast to the essentially abstract nature of Edna's quest. Through music she discovers a kindred spirit in Edna, whose vision of the naked man occurs shortly before the musician plays a Chopin Impromptu that arouses Edna's passions and brings her to tears. "Mademoiselle Reisz perceived her agitation. . . . She patted her . . . upon the shoulder as she said: 'You are the only one worth playing for. Those others? Bah!'" (p. 27). She realizes that for her young friend music is the correlative of passion just as it is for her, but once their relationship develops Mademoiselle Reisz discovers that Edna's sensitivity does not encompass the discipline or the clarity of vision requisite to either the artist or the rebel. This is made clear one afternoon when Edna explains that she is becoming an artist. The older woman responds harshly, saying that "You have pretensions, Madame . . . to succeed, the artist must possess the courageous soul . . . that dares and defies" (p. 63). . . .

Mademoiselle Reisz functions as the only example of a free, independent woman whose hardiness Edna must emulate if she is to succeed and soar above "tradition and prejudice." There is no question that the older woman provides Edna with a more viable model than Adèle Ratignolle, who is, after all, trapped without even knowing it. Mademoiselle Reisz's apartment becomes a refuge for Edna, and the pianist comes closer than anyone else to making contact and supplying advice that could be helpful as Edna tries to find a place for her new self in the world. Nevertheless, her role in the novel is problematic, for she is an imperfect model whose positive qualities are balanced by abrasiveness and egocentrism. Chopin calls attention to the musician's idiosyncrasies when she introduces her into the story. Robert has gone to ask her to play for his mother's guests and finds her in one of the cottages: "She was dragging a chair in and out of her room, and at intervals objecting to the crying of a baby, which a nurse in the adjoining cottage was endeavoring to put to sleep. She was a disagreeable little woman, no longer young, who had quarreled with almost every one, owing to a temper which was self-assertive and a disposition to trample upon the rights of others" (p. 26). Later, at Edna's dinner party, "Mademoiselle had only disagreeable things to say of the symphony concerts, and insulting remarks to make of all the musicians of New Orleans, singly and collectively" (p. 87). While Edna instinctively rebels against the larger social dictates of Creole society, those social graces that express less overwhelming *convenances* are still important to her, so that her amusement at her friend's disdain of conventions does not mean that she intends to imitate her. More subtly, Mademoiselle Reisz fails as a model because at this point Edna's passions, unlike her friend's, cannot be sublimated to music, but need physical expression. Like all her friends, Mademoiselle Reisz is eventually left behind as Edna increasingly dissociates herself from society and moves further into the mazes of solitude.

Sandra M. Gilbert on Edna As
an Aphrodite Figure

The oceanic imagery embedded in Chopin's description of Edna's response to Mlle. Reisz's music is neither casual nor coincidental; rather it suggests yet another agency through which Mme. Le Brun's predominantly female summer colony on Grand Isle awakens and empowers this Creole Bovary. For Chopin's Aphrodite, like Hesiod's, is born from the sea, and born specifically because the colony where she comes to consciousness is situated, like so many places that are significant for women, outside patriarchal culture, beyond the limits of the city where men make history, on one of those magical shores that mark the margin where nature intersects with culture. Here power can flow from outside, from the timelessness or from, in Mircea Eliade's phrase, the "Great Time" that is free of historical constraints; and here, therefore, the sea can speak in a seductive voice, "never ceasing, whispering, clamoring, murmuring, inviting the soul to wander for a spell in abysses of solitude; to lose itself in mazes of inward contemplation" (chap. 6).

It is significant, then, that not only Edna's silent dialogue with Mlle. Reisz but also her confessional conversation with Adèle Ratignolle incorporates sea imagery. Reconstructing her first childhood sense of self for her friend, Edna remembers "a meadow that seemed as big as the ocean" in which as a little girl she "threw out her arms as if swimming when she walked, beating the tall grass as one strikes out in the water" (chap. 7). Just as significantly she speculates that, as she journeyed through this seemingly endless grass, she was most likely "running away from prayers, from the Presbyterian service, read in a spirit of gloom by my father that chills me yet to think of." She was running away, that is, from the dictations and interdictions of patriarchal culture, especially of patriarchal theology, and running into the wild openness of nature. Even so early, the story implies, her quest for an alternative theology, or at least for an alternative mythology, had begun. In the summer of her awakening on Grand Isle, that quest is extended into the more formalized process of learning not to run but to swim.

Edna's education in swimming is, of course, obviously symbolic, representing as it does both a positive political lesson in staying afloat and an ambiguously valuable sentimental education in the consequences of getting in over one's head. More important, however, is the fact that swimming immerses Edna in an *other* element—an element, indeed, of otherness—in whose baptismal embrace she is mystically and mythically revitalized, renewed, reborn. That Chopin wants specifically to emphasize this aspect of Edna's education in swimming, moreover, is made clear by the magical occasion on which her heroine's first independent swim takes place. Following Mlle. Reisz's evocative concert, "someone, perhaps it was Robert [Edna's lover-to-be], thought of a bath at that mystic hour and under that mystic moon." Appropriately, then, on this night that sits "lightly upon the sea and land," this night when "the white light of the moon [has] fallen upon the world like the mystery and softness of sleep," the previously timid Edna begins for the first time to swim, feeling "as if some power of significant import had been given her" and aspiring "to swim far out, where no woman had swum before" (chap. 10). Her new strength and her new ambition are symbolically fostered by the traditionally female mythic associations of moonlight and water, as well as by the romantic attendance of Robert Le Brun and the seemingly erotic "heavy perfume of a field of white blossoms somewhere near." At the same time, however, Chopin's description of the waves breaking on the beach "in little foamy crests ... like slow white serpents" suggests that Edna is swimming not only with new powers but into a kind of alternative paradise, one that depends upon deliberate inversions and conversions of conventional theological images, while her frequent reminders that this sea is a gulf reinforce our sense that its waters are at least as metaphysical as those of, say, the Golfo Placido in Conrad's *Nostromo*. Thus, even more important than Edna's swim are both its narrative and its aesthetic consequences, twin textual transformations that

56

influence and energize the rest of Chopin's novel. For in swimming away from the beach where her prosaic husband watches and waits, Edna swims away from the shore of her old life, where she had lingered for twenty-eight years, hesitant and ambivalent. As she swims, moreover, she swims not only toward a female paradise but out of one kind of novel—the work of Eliotian or Flaubertian "realism" she had previously inhabited—and into a new kind of work, a mythic/metaphysical romance that elaborates her distinctively female fantasy of paradisiacal fulfillment and therefore adumbrates much of the feminist modernism that was to come within a few decades.

Rosemary F. Franklin on Mythical Elements in Edna's Story

In many ways *The Awakening* is a critique of romantic love. Chopin understands that sometimes the animus in the woman is so strongly projected onto the beloved that she cannot perceive the real man. Mlle Reisz understands projection too as she asks Edna if she loves Robert. Edna responds, saying a woman does not select nor can she know why she loves (26). Even Edna, like a tragic hero, knows her weakness— succumbing to "infatuation"—because she had been infatuated as a girl with three men, and the "hopelessness" of these loves colored them "with the lofty tones of a great passion" (7). But she persists in loving Robert, especially since he is gone, and only when he returns from Mexico does she allow herself to perceive briefly that some of the romance wanes because he is with her (33).

As the stimulus to Edna's awakening, Robert is the most important Eros figure in the novel, and after he leaves for Mexico, because, like Eros, he fears the collective, Edna must begin the lonely labor to find herself. Alcée and Victor are two other faces of Eros. Alcée, the promiscuous aspect of Eros, bears a wound from a duel over love and describes himself as "a wicked, ill-disciplined boy" (25). That Edna has an affair with him even as she knows Robert is returning demonstrates that lust is a small part of her love for Robert. Victor is a more innocent Alcée. This high-spirited, youthful Eros plays the role at Edna's party, where he is draped and bedecked with roses and where Gouvernail quotes from Swinburne on desire (30). Significantly, all these men revolve around the matriarchs, who keep them more or less under control.

After Edna returns to New Orleans, she must embark on Psyche's task of developing her strengths. She resumes painting, but before art can enable her to find herself, she must deal with the moods that arise from her discontent and her romantic fantasies. Warned by Mlle Reisz, Edna needs to grow strong wings to fly above the "plain of tradition and prejudice." She engages in a "quest"—Chopin's word—to gain advice from her friends, but her quest for knowledge about her self is mixed in with her desire to gain information about Robert. Here she again traces Psyche's pattern. Instead of pursuing positive labors, however, Edna seems to be consuming psychic energy fighting despondency. Adèle's marriage depresses her, and at the Lebruns' house she almost gives up her quest when she finds Robert has not mentioned her in letters.

Edna's birthday party marks a significant moment for her. It is a private coming of age since she plans to move into the "pigeon house." The narrative voice strikes a triumphant tone as it describes her as "the regal woman, the one who rules, who looks on, who stands alone," but almost immediately despair strikes her: "she felt the old ennui overtaking her; the hopelessness which so often assailed her, which came upon her like an obsession. . . . a chill breath . . . seemed to issue from some vast cavern wherein discords wailed" (30). She thinks of the "unattainable" beloved and begins a journey down into her own Hades, dressed almost like Persephone, goddess of the underworld.

Edna's mood persists as the novel rapidly draws to a close. After she and Robert have revealed their love for each other, Robert is frightened by her determination to manage her own life because he is still very much a creature of the collective. He definitively separates from her for the second and last time. Ironically, the hold of the matriarchy over Edna is also evident as she leaves Robert to attend Adèle's delivery. Adèle's physical labor distracts Edna from the spiritual labor in which she is engaged. She leaves the "scene of torture" with Adèle's warning in her mind—"Think of the children" (37). Not only must Edna remember her duty to her present children, but she may also be thinking of some possible future children if she lives her life as a sexually liberated woman. These thoughts are amplified as Dr. Mandelet expresses his opinion that romantic love is nature's trick to secure mothers for the race. Edna's awakening to the illusion of romantic love is reinforced by Robert's departure. As the night passes, she realizes that no man will ever satisfy her restless soul. She can never return to the dark palace where perfect union with the beloved is imaginable, and she is unable to engage in the true labors to find her self. The loneliness of the solitary soul engulfs her as the powerful unintegrated contents of the unconscious win.

Barbara H. Solomon on Characters as Foils to Edna

One of the most fertile topics for . . . exploration in Kate Chopin's *The Awakening* is the author's brilliant use of major and minor characters as foils for Edna Pontellier. As Edna undergoes a crisis, during her twenty-eighth year, in which her previous identity as Léonce Pontellier's submissive and passionless wife is transformed into that of a rebellious, passionate neophyte artist, she consciously judges the women around her, especially Adèle Ratignolle and Mlle Reisz, as she seeks to understand her own needs and actions. But in addition to the substantial depictions of these two characters, Chopin sketches a series of impressionistic portraits of minor characters who dramatize Edna's problems and options. These foils range from the shadowy pair of lovers who are vacationing at Grand Isle and who never speak to any of the other guests to the sensual and provocative Mariequita and, back in New Orleans, the sophisticated Mrs. Highcamp. Though each is very different, all share an important dramatic role. Through their attitudes or behavior, they illuminate the inevitable results of certain ideas and choices that occur to Edna at various times.

The lovers who appear early in the novel are always pictured by Chopin as backdrop figures. They live for each other, leaving when other characters appear and eschewing the life of the community of families that has grown up around Mrs. Lebrun's hotel. Chopin emphasizes their isolation. . . .

When, late in the novel, Edna declares to Robert that she cares nothing for Léonce Pontellier and suggests that she and Robert will be able to be together, she is, in fact, suggesting that they should turn their backs on the community of family and friends who would be scandalized by such a liaison. Edna believes, or wants to believe, that she and Robert can live for each other without concern for anybody else. Her dream can be summarized by that most romantic phrase, giving up "all for love." But the relationship that Edna proposes must lead to their alienation from the comfortable Creole world to which both now very much belong. They would indeed become like the insubstantial lovers who exclude themselves from the activities of the world.

Next, two portraits of women instruct the reader about the limitations of Edna's choices. The first, Mariequita, is the "young barefooted Spanish girl" who makes the boat trip from Grand Isle to the Chênière Caminada with Edna and Robert on the Sunday when they spend the entire day together. . . .

Edna's obvious curiosity makes Mariequita self-conscious. There is a frankly sensual quality about this girl, who knows Robert and begins to question him. When Mariequita asks whether Edna is Robert's "sweetheart," he responds, "She's a married lady, and has two children." His answer clearly begs the question, one that Robert probably has not yet asked himself. But Mariequita's rejoinder comically prefigures the serious situation that Robert and Edna must face. "Oh! well!" she says, "Francisco ran away with Sylvano's wife, who had four children. They took all his money and one of the children and stole his boat" (12). Ironically, only a few minutes later, Robert tells Edna about his plan of patching and trimming his own boat, fantasizing that he and she can go sailing together "some night in the pirogue when the moon shines." But Edna could never adopt Mariequita's casual attitude toward marriage and infidelity, much as she struggles to escape the consequences of her unfortunate marriage to Léonce. Edna may not care whether her behavior hurts her husband, but she is haunted by her fear of the harm she might cause her small sons, Etienne and Raoul. . . .

Mariequita's comments point up the contrast in the two women's attitudes, emphasizing the sense of entrapment that Edna increasingly comes to feel as the novel progresses.

A much more sophisticated woman, Mrs. James Highcamp, serves as a second foil who dramatizes the impossibility of a certain kind of future for Edna. Early in the novel, when Léonce notices Mrs. Highcamp's calling card among the other cards of the visitors who had paid a call on one of Edna's Tuesdays at home (only to find her out for the afternoon), he comments, "[T]he less you have to do with Mrs. Highcamp, the better." Significantly, when Léonce is away and Edna has begun to live as she pleases, without regard for her husband's ideas, Edna becomes somewhat friendly with this acquaintance, dining at her house and attending the races with her and Alcée Arobin. Chopin portrays Mrs. Highcamp as a wife and mother who flirts with attractive men and makes a mockery of her marriage: "Mrs. Highcamp was a worldly but unaffected, intelligent, slim, tall blonde in the forties, with an indifferent manner and blue eyes that stared. She had a daughter who served her as a pretext for cultivating the society of young men of fashion" (25).

At the birthday dinner that Edna gives just before leaving Léonce's house for her "pigeon house," Mrs. Highcamp is seated next to Victor Lebrun. . . .

During the course of the evening's festivities, she weaves a garland of yellow and red roses that she places on Victor's head; then she drapes her white silk scarf gracefully around him. When Mrs. Highcamp encourages Victor to sing, he chooses the song that Edna associates with her love for Robert. As Mrs. Highcamp departs, she invites Victor to call on her daughter, ostensibly so that the two young people can enjoy speaking French and singing French songs together. Victor responds that he intends to visit Mrs. Highcamp "at the first opportunity which presented itself." Obviously, under the guise of providing company for her daughter, Mrs. Highcamp intends to pursue this young man for her own needs. . . .

Edna specifically rejects Mrs. Highcamp's way of life in the closing passages of the novel after she realizes that Robert will not return because of his Creole code of honor concerning infidelity and adultery. Without Robert, she visualizes a pattern for satisfying her sensual needs that the reader recognizes might well parallel Mrs. Highcamp's behavior with men: "[Edna] had said over and over to herself: 'To-day it is Arobin; to-morrow it will be some one else. It makes no difference to me, it doesn't matter about Léonce Pontellier—but Raoul and Etienne!'" (39). Having experienced passion and being unwilling to lead a life deprived of such experiences, Edna is also unwilling to lead a life of barely concealed subterfuge such as that of Mrs. Highcamp. . . .

Chopin's use of other women as foils for her central character fulfills three distinct functions. First, since Edna is not particularly analytical—at one point in the novel she thinks that she needs to set aside time soon to try to determine what sort of person she truly is—her interaction with foils such as Adèle and Mlle Reisz enables the reader to better compare Edna's character and goals with those of other women. Second, Chopin's sympathetic depiction of these two very different foils suggests the considerable range of women's behavior during an era in which women were frequently categorized as similar in instincts and interests: creatures in need of domestic security and comfort. And, finally, Edna's interaction with Adèle, who implores her to consider the children, and with Mlle Reisz, who encourages Edna to soar freely as an artist and to pursue her relationship with Robert, helps to convince readers that Edna's problems are insoluble given the environment, the era, and the strength of her newly discovered, uncompromising identity.

ELIZABETH AMMONS ON WHITE LIBERATION/BLACK OPPRESSION IN *THE AWAKENING*

The background of *The Awakening* is filled with nameless, faceless black women carefully categorized as black, mulatto, quadroon, and Griffe, distinctions which, significantly, do not even show up in Alice Dunbar-Nelson's book.[1] Also, Mexican American and Mexican women play crucial subordinate roles in *The Awakening*. Taken together, all of these women of color make Edna Pontellier's "liberation" possible. As menials they free her from work, from cooking to childcare. As prostitutes they service/educate the men in her world. Chopin is both in and out of control of this political story.

Compared to a Thomas Nelson Page or Thomas Dixon, Kate Chopin had liberal, enlightened views on the subject of race.[2] One of the ways that she shows how despicable Victor Lebrun is, for example, is by providing glimpses of his racism—his contempt for black people in general, his verbal abuse of the black woman who insists on doing her job of opening the door when Edna knocks, his arrogant assumption of credit for the silver and gold cake which he orders two black women to create in his kitchen. It is also possible to argue that, as Edna awakens, black characters change from nameless parts of the scenery to individuals with names and voices. On Grand Isle the blacks who tend white women's children, carry messages, sweep porches, and crouch on the floor to work the treadle of Madame Lebrun's sewing machine (a child does this) so that Madame's health is not imperiled move through the narrative speechless and nameless. As the book progresses, however, individuals emerge: the "boy" Joe who works for the Pontelliers in the city, the "mulatresse" Catiche to whose tiny garden restaurant in the suburbs Edna repairs, the capable "Griffe" nurse who sees Madame Ratignolle through the birth of her baby. Yet as even these mentions betray, the individual people of color who do emerge from the background, as the book traces Edna's increasing distance from the rigid class- and gender-bound world of her marriage, are finally no more than types, human categories—unexamined representatives of the novel's repressed African American context. Minor white characters are not identified by the cups of Irish or French or German blood in them. In other words, even an argument that claims progression in the individualization of black characters has to face the fact that images of black people in *The Awakening*, a book about a woman trying to escape a limiting, caging assignment of gender that stunts her humanity and robs her of choices, are stereotypic and demeaning.

Deeper is the problem that the very liberation about which the book fantasizes is purchased on the backs of black women. If Edna's children did not have a hired "quadroon" to care for them night and day, it is extremely unlikely that she would swim off into the sunset at the end of *The Awakening* in a glorious burst of Emersonian free will. Edna's story is not universal, although most feminist literary criticism has failed to acknowledge the fact. It is the story of a woman of one race and class who is able to dream of total personal freedom because an important piece of that highly individualistic ideal (itself the product of the very capitalism that Edna in some ways gropes to shed) has already been bought for her. Though she does not see it, her freedom comes at the expense of women of other races and a lower class, whose namelessness, facelessness, and voicelessness record a much more profound oppression in *The Awakening* than does the surface story of Edna Pontellier. The great examined story of *The Awakening* is its heroine's break for freedom. The great unexamined story, one far more disturbing than the fiction privileged in the text, is the narrative of sororal oppression across race and class.

Toni Morrison argues in her groundbreaking essay "Unspeakable Things Unspoken: The Afro-American Presence in American Literature" that it is not the why but the how of racial erasure that constitutes the truly important question: "What intellectual feats had to be performed by the author or his critic to erase me from a society seething with my presence, and what effect has that performance had on the work?"[3] The answer to this question in *The Awakening* is in one way quite simple. The repression of black women's stories—and with them Edna's identity as oppressor as well as oppressed—plunges not just Edna but also Chopin into a killing silence from which neither returns. It is widely agreed that Kate Chopin did not write much after *The Awakening* because the hostile reviews of the novel devastated her. I am sure that is true. One might ask, however, after *The Awakening*, unless Chopin was willing to confront race, what was there to say? The book brilliantly spins the privileged white female fantasy of utter and complete personal freedom out to its end, which is oblivion—the sea, death. The fantasy itself deadends. (Willa Cather's irritation with the novel, which she criticized for its "over-idealization of love" and its shallowly "expecting an individual and self-limited passion to yield infinite variety, pleasure, and distraction," does not seem so cranky when viewed from this perspective.[4] Cut off from the large, urgent, ubiquitous struggle for freedom of African Americans in Chopin's America, a struggle hinted at but repeatedly repressed in the text, the utterly individualistic and solipsistic white female fantasy of freedom that *The Awakening* indulges in can only end in silence—in death.

Notes

1. New Orleans-born Alice Dunbar-Nelson (1875–1935), widely published author of poems, short fiction, art and literary criticism, and essays on history and culture, stands as a transitional figure between African-American writers of an earlier generation (including her first husband, Paul Lawrence Dunbar) and the artists/writers of the Harlem Renaissance. Ammons has been discussing Dunbar-Nelson's *The Goodness of St. Rocque and Other Stories*. In her "People of Color in Louisiana," *Journal of Negro History* 1 (October 1916): 361, Dunbar-Nelson writes:

> The title of a possible discussion of the Negro in Louisiana presents difficulties, for there is no such word as Negro permissible in speaking of this State. The history of the State is filled with attempts to define, sometimes at the point of the sword, oftenest in civil or criminal courts, the meaning of the word Negro. By common consent, it came to mean in Louisiana, prior to 1865, slave, and after the war, those whose complexions were noticeably dark. As Grace King so delightfully puts it, "The pure-blooded African was never called colored, but always Negro." The *gens de couleur*, colored people, were always a class apart, separated from and superior to the Negroes, ennobled

were it only by one drop of white blood in their veins. The caste seems to have existed from the first introduction of slaves. To the whites, all Africans who were not of pure blood were *gens de couleur*. Among themselves, however, there were jealous and fiercely-guarded distinctions: "griffes, briques, mulattoes, quadroons, octoroons, each term meaning one degree's further transfiguration toward the Caucasian standard of physical perfection" (Grace King, *New Orleans, the Place and the People During the Ancien Regime* [New York, 1895] 333).

2. Discussion of the treatment of race in Chopin's work can be found in Seyersted, *Kate Chopin*, and in Anne Goodwyn Jones's excellent chapter on Chopin in *Tomorrow Is Another Day: The Woman Writer in the South, 1859–1936* (Baton Rouge: Louisiana State University Press, 1981), pp. 135–84. [See above, p. 299, n. 3. Thomas Dixon (1864–1946), North Carolina writer best known for *The Clansman* (1905), which was made into the movie *Birth of a Nation*—Editor.]

3. Toni Morrison, "Unspeakable Things Unspoken: The Afro-American Presence in American Literature," *Michigan Quarterly Review*, 28 (Winter 1989), 12.

4. See above, pp. 170–72 [Editor].

MARGO CULLEY ON THE SOCIAL/HISTORICAL BACKGROUND OF *THE AWAKENING*

The 1890s in America was a decade of social change and social tension. The depression of 1893–96 accentuated class divisions, and urbanization and industrialization continued to challenge traditional ways of life. The World's Columbian Exposition in Chicago in 1893 announced the fact of the machine age in a dramatic, public fashion. Darwinism and higher criticism of the Bible threatened established ways of thinking about human origins and destiny. The 1890s also brought legalized segregation, or Jim Crow laws, to the South. . . .

By 1890 "the woman question" had been a matter of public discussion in America for over fifty years. In that year, the two national suffrage organizations merged for the final push for the vote—which would not come, however, for another thirty years. . . .

Women's independence became a central theme in the fiction of Kate Chopin, though she herself was never active in any suffrage organization and was even known to make fun of women's clubs. Strongly committed to personal freedom, Chopin defied social convention in numerous ways, including smoking cigarettes, riding horseback in bright-colored costume, walking about the village and city alone, running her husband's business for a time after his death, refusing to remarry, and likely taking lovers. Her diary records that she met one of the Claflin sisters while on her honeymoon and assured her that she would never fall into "the useless degrading life of most married ladies.[2]

Most married women in Louisiana, where *The Awakening* is set, were the legal property of their husbands. In the late nineteenth century, the Napoleonic code was still the basis of state law governing the marriage contract. Though she might retain control over any inheritances she had received prior to her marriage, all of a wife's "accumulations" after marriage were the property of her husband, including any money she might earn and the clothes she wore. The husband was the legal guardian of the children and until 1855 was granted custody of the children in the event of a divorce. The wife was "bound to live with her husband, and follow him wherever he [chose] to reside." A wife could not sign any legal contract (with the exception of her will) without the consent of her husband, nor could she institute a lawsuit, appear in court, hold public office, or make a donation to a living person. The woman's position in the eyes of the law is well captured in Article 1591 of the laws of Louisiana: "The following persons are absolutely incapable of bearing witness to testaments: 1. Woman of any age whatsoever. 2. Male children who have not attained the age of sixteen years complete. 3. Persons who are insane, deaf, dumb or blind. 4. Persons whom the criminal laws declare incapable of exercising civil functions." Though divorce laws in Louisiana were somewhat more liberal than those in other parts of the country—divorce could be granted on the grounds of abandonment after one year of separation—divorce rates were much lower than in other states. Louisiana was a largely Catholic state, and divorce was a scandalous and rather rare occurrence (twenty-nine divorces granted per one hundred thousand members of the population in 1890). In any case, Chopin's Edna Pontellier had no legal grounds for divorce, though her husband undoubtedly did. . . .

The New Orleans *Daily Picayune* was the first major American newspaper edited by a woman, and its pages supported a variety of women's causes in the 1890s. Reference to "the New Woman," the late-nineteenth-century equivalent of "the liberated woman," appeared often in its pages. A June 1897 article recounts the occupations that women in the city were pursuing: "Among other things gleaned from the city directory of our own city, is the fact that there are two women barbers, following the hirsute tradition in the Crescent City. There are also importers of cigars among the fair sex, six women undertakers, one embalmer, a real estate agent (it is true in partnership with a man), insurance solicitors, several practicing physicians, a box manufacturer, three drummers, a steamboat captain, several florists and a number of liquor dealers." The national census of 1890 showed that in only 9 of the 369 professions listed for the city were women not represented

These social changes serve as the broad backdrop to *The Awakening* and, in part, explain the avalanche of hostile criticism that the novel received. When Kate Chopin created a fictional hero who would test the limits of freedom for a woman of her social class, she touched a very raw nerve of the body politic. Though Kate Chopin had not lived in New Orleans for twenty years when she wrote *The Awakening*, her visits to Louisiana had made her very aware of change. When she strategically placed her Edna Pontellier in an aristocratic Creole society, she knew it to be much under siege from the newer entrepreneurial society of "American" New Orleans. Chopin also knew, as did her readers, that the privileged, leisured world of Grand Isle where the novel opens had been literally destroyed by a hurricane in 1893, a nice image of "the storm" of social ferment that was leaving America and American women forever changed.[3] When she published her bold novel, Chopin should not have been surprised to find herself caught in the eye of that storm.

Notes

2. Per Seversted, *Kate Chopin: A Critical Biography* (Baton Rouge: Louisiana State UP, 1969), 33. The woman Chopin met was either Victoria Claflin Woodhull (1838–1927) or her sister Tennessee Claflin Cook (1845–1923), journalists, businesswomen, spiritualists, advocates of women's rights including suffrage, dress reform, legalized prostitution, and "free love." In 1872 Victoria Woodhull ran for president of the United States as the nominee of the People's Party.

3. See Helen Taylor, *Gender, Race and Region in the Writings of Grace King, Ruth McEnery Stuart, and Kate Chopin* (Baton Rouge: Louisiana State UP, 1989, 177–78). Also Frederick Stielow, "Grand Isle, Louisiana, and the 'New' Leisure, 1866–1893," *Louisiana History* 23 (1982): 239–57.

KATHRYN LEE SEIDEL ON EDNA'S PAINTING

When reading *The Awakening*, one is so struck by Edna Pontellier's overwhelming discovery of her own sexuality that it is easy to overlook her artistic awakening and her attempts to nurture her creative ability. Edna appears to have the economic prerequisites that Woolf defines as essential to the artist: as the wife of a wealthy man she has income, she has servants to cook and provide child care, and she has ample education. She has time, space, and money, and despite the impediments to her development as a painter voiced by her family and friends, she develops nonetheless. The growth of her art is characterized by three distinct stages: her early mimetic work that reinforces the paternalistic values of her culture; her rebellious portraits; and her daring, original drawings that she creates after moving into her own house. . . .

Edna's initial motive for creating art is not merely to have a pastime but to engage in a positive, pleasurable endeavor. Moreover, she begins to wish to improve. Selecting Madame Ratignolle as her subject, Edna proceeds to attempt to imitate the great masters by perceiving her as a "sensuous Madonna" (891). Her choice of her close friend as her model, depicted in a conventional pictorial mode, is well within the accepted subjects for a woman painter. . . .

Adèle Ratignolle . . . is disappointed that the work does not look like herself; she expected a mimetic, realistic drawing. Is her comment one that indicates Edna's flawed technique, or is Edna attempting a more impressionist sketch? Edna said she wished to capture the Madonna-like essence of Adèle, so Edna's purpose was not photographic realism. When Edna then crumples the sketch, she does not do so because it does not look like Adèle or because Adèle criticized it; her reason is that the sketch does not capture this intangible quality. In the 19th century, European and American painting was challenging the tradition of mimetic realism. The impressionists were already known throughout America, and it is likely that Chopin's intellectual circle was well aware of their work. . . .

Not only does Edna's technique bring criticism from Adèle, but she also urges a conventional motive for painting. Adèle's concept of the proper role for the woman artist is expressed in her own pleasant piano accompaniment, which she says is "a means of brightening the home and making it attractive" (904). To her, the role of art for women is domestic decoration. In this Adèle and Léonce Pontellier, Edna's husband, agree absolutely—the Pontellier house is filled with paintings and statues that give him the "genuine pleasure" of having "bought" and possessed them (931). Pontellier becomes angry because Edna's increasing devotion of her time to art removes her from the family and also because her claim to privacy prevents her art from accruing to the inventory of his possessions. Moreover, her physical absence annoys him because he believes Edna must be physically available to him at all times—recall the scene in chapter III in which he awakens Edna in order to chat about his day. Pontellier regards her body as his to command; Edna's desire to paint is an assertion that she wishes to own her own body. Edna wishes to possess her art, not give it to her husband to possess and display, just as she wishes to regard her body as her own. . . .

In her bright and cheerful atelier, she now works with "great energy and interest" (939), exploring new subjects for her art. She first paints her children, then the "quadroon" maid, then the housemaid whom Edna perceives has a "back and shoulders

... molded on classic lines," and whose "hair, loosened from its confining cap, became an inspiration" (940). These choices are increasingly bold, a far cry from the fictitious and stereotypical Bavarian peasants she gave to Adèle. Moreover, the loosening of the maid's hair suggests the physical freedom Edna feels as well as her increasing sense of power over her models and materials. . . .

As Edna comes closer to an adulterous relationship with Alcée Arobin, she becomes more experimental with her painting. No longer interested in the safe content for women's art—scenery and portraits of friends—she attempts to sketch her dour Calvinistic father. Chopin gives an original account of the female artist with the male model: under Edna's gaze, her father sits "rigid and unflinching, as he had faced the cannon's mouth in days gone by" (950). The comparison of his facing Edna to facing a cannon reveals that, metaphorically, Edna as an artist has power and control over him, a situation much changed from her meekness with him when she was a child. The fact that he faces the cannon's *mouth* suggests Edna could devour him if she chose, a metaphor for women's power. Moreover, her ability to render her father motionless echoes the myth of the Medusa, whose gaze paralyzes men who see her. By painting her father, Edna gains the ability to define him, to control his image before the world. Perhaps because they are at last on an equal footing, the sessions allow Edna to feel warmly toward her father for the first time in her life and her art begins a process of healing the rift between them. . . .

Throughout *The Awakening*, Edna takes positive, aggressive actions to learn her art, even in the face of hostile critics. She improves as an artist, and with her portraits of her father and her lover, achieves an autonomy and control over them and herself, a self-assurance she does not usually have in the other aspects of her life. Ultimately, however, for Edna not artistic expression nor love, friendship, or sex can reconcile her creativity, her personal growth, the expectations of her society, and her own tortured sense of self. When she acts as an artist she feels her strength, but she cannot transfer this knowledge to other aspects of her life.

The heroine of *The Awakening* borrows the rhetoric of self-ownership when she vows she will "never again belong to another than herself" (100). But in Edna Pontellier's attempt to take possession of herself, Kate Chopin unpacks the paradoxical logic of self-ownership in all its contradiction and impossibility. It is through her role as the wife—and marital property—of Léonce Pontellier that Edna first looks for a self she might possess; and it is as a mother that Edna declares her resolve to withhold some part of that self from the claims of others. In her aspiration to self-ownership, Edna claims title to a self that exists only in relation to her status as the property of others.

As the novel opens, Edna's husband, a wealthy New Orleans stockbroker who has brought his family to an exclusive summer resort, surveys his wife like "property": "'You are burnt beyond recognition' [Léonce says], looking at his wife as one looks at a valuable piece of personal property which has suffered some damage" (21). Léonce's comment is both the reader's introduction to Edna and Edna's introduction to herself: for in response to Léonce's anxiety, Edna makes her first self-examination in this novel about a heroine who is "beginning to realize her position in the universe as a human being, and to recognize her relations as an individual to the world within and about her" (31–32).

Edna, having been told "you are burnt beyond recognition,"

> held up her hands, strong, shapely hands, and surveyed them critically, drawing up her lawn sleeves above the wrists. Looking at them reminded her of her rings, which she had given to her husband before leaving for the beach. She silently reached out to him and he, understanding, took the rings from his vest pocket and dropped them into her open palm. She slipped them upon her fingers. (21)

In the context of the property system in which Edna exists as a sign of value, her body is detachable and alienable from her own viewpoint: the hands and wrists are part of the body yet can be objectified, held out and examined as if they belonged to someone else—as indeed, in some sense that Léonce insists on very literally, they do belong to someone else. Edna's perception of her own body is structured by the detachability of the hand and arm as signs of Léonce's ownership of her. Her hands also suggest the possibility of being an owner herself when they make the proprietary gesture of reaching out for the rings that Léonce obediently drops into the palm (this gesture of Edna's contrasts with a bride's conventional passive reception of the ring). The hands are the organs of appropriation: Elizabeth Cady Stanton, in a speech on female rights given in 1892, argued that "to deny [to woman] the rights of property is like cutting off the hands."[1] In having Edna put on the rings herself (a gesture she will again perform at a moment when she decisively turns away from her domestic role), Chopin suggests that the chief item of property owned by the proprietary Edna is Edna herself. Thus the opening scene foreshadows the turning point of the plot, when Edna, deciding to leave Léonce's house, resolves "never again to belong to another than herself" (100). . . .

Chopin's dramatization of female self-ownership demonstrates the central importance of the ideology of woman's value in exchange to contemporary notions of female selfhood. If, as Stanton declares, "in discussing the rights of woman, we are to consider, first, what belongs to her as an individual" (247), what Edna Pontellier considers as her property is, first, her body. Her body is both what she owns and what she owns with. She begins to discover a self by uncovering her hands and "surveying them critically" with her eyes, thus making an appropriate visual assessment of herself as a proprietary being. Her hands and eyes will serve her in her "venture" into the "work" of sketching and painting (75). Thus her hands, by remaining attached (and not cut off like those of the woman who is denied the rights of property), serve her visual appropriation of the world and provide the first object of this appropriation: her own body.

Edna's hands appear in two states: naked and sunburned, and ringed. In the first state, they are conventionally "unrecognizable" as signs of her status as Léonce's wife. Sunburned hands, by indicating the performance of outdoor labor, would nullify Edna's "value" as a sign of Léonce's wealth. . . .

Thus Edna's hands, in their naked and exposed state, serve as a reminder of Léonce's property interest while they also suggest an identity and proprietary interests of her own. . . .

Edna's death in the ocean dramatizes the self-ownership rhetoric of Elizabeth Cady Stanton. Stanton argues that "self-sovereignty" is the existential birthright of both women and men, for every human being "launched on the sea of life" is unique and "alone" (248). But women's self-sovereignty specifically denotes sexual self-determination. And Stanton insists that women—that is, mothers—earn a special presumptive self-sovereignty, for "alone [woman] goes to the gates of death to give life to every man that is born into the world; no one can share her fears, no one can mitigate her pangs; and if her sorrow is greater than she can bear, alone she passes beyond the gates into the vast unknown" (251). At the moment of extreme maternal giving, the moment when motherhood takes her life, the woman owns her self by withholding herself from motherhood.

Note

1. Stanton, 249. In this speech Stanton gave in 1892 on the occasion of her resignation from the presidency of the suffrage movement, woman's entitlement to a full complement of civil rights stems from her aloneness and existential "self-sovereignty." The female self Stanton evokes is an absolute, possessive self whose metaphorical situation is that of a lone individual "on a solitary island" or "launched on the sea of life." *The Awakening*'s original title was *A Solitary Soul*, and in Chopin's novel, as in Stanton's rhetoric, female subjectivity and women's rights are grounded in absolute and irreducible selfhood. For an account of early English feminists' commitment to absolute selfhood, see Gallagher 1988.

EMILY TOTH ON MISREADING *THE AWAKENING*

Sex is a major barrier. Modern readers expect more graphic language, and are prone to misunderstand the intimacies they do see. There is, for instance, *The Awakening*'s chapter VII, in which Edna and Madame Adèle Ratignolle, both handsome women who enjoy each other's company, go down to the beach together at Grand Isle. That summer, Edna has been startled by the Creole "absence of prudery," and especially by Adèle's comforting, caressing touches. Readers a century later, confusing sexuality and sensuality, sometimes see more than what is there—and think there is a "lesbian" connection between the two.

There is indeed, if "lesbian" means love between women, or what Chopin calls, in that chapter, "the subtle bond which we call sympathy, which we might as well call love." But the word "lesbian" was not in common use in Chopin's day: women who loved women were not put in a separate category under a different label. In the 1890s Edna and Adèle are, in Chopin's terms, "intimate friends." That does not mean what it would mean, bluntly, a century later—a genital connection. It does mean a unique and sometimes wordless emotional and spiritual understanding, the kind that unlocks Edna's thoughts about herself.

There are other things in *The Awakening* that are still to be unlocked—such as the sexual orientation of Robert, Edna's summer cavalier. He is definitely different from the other fellows. They all smoke cigars, manly and phallic; Robert smokes cigarettes, as women do (he claims they're cheaper). The other men hold jobs in the city, while Robert hangs about with his mother and attaches himself to a different unattainable—usually married—woman every summer. Clean-shaven and light-haired, he resembles Edna, and the husbands regard him as a safe puppy dog. But Adèle Ratignolle, more discerning, asks Robert to leave her friend Edna alone. Edna is an outsider: "She is not one of us; she is not like us. She might make the unfortunate blunder of taking you seriously" (VIII).

When Robert objects that he is not a clown or a jack-in-the-box, Adèle gives an even stronger hint about what he really is: "If your attentions to any married women here were ever offered with any intention of being convincing, you would not be the gentleman we all know you to be, and you would be unfit to associate with the wives and daughters of the people who trust you."

Not long after that, and without consulting Edna, Robert flees to Mexico.

Before he leaves, though, Robert encounters Mr. Pontellier in the city, and Edna wonders if he seemed "gay." Her husband says Robert was cheerful, which is "natural in a young man about to seek his fortune and adventure in a strange, queer country" (XVI).

When Robert returns, he has a pouch embroidered by—he says—a girl in Vera Cruz. But homosexual male Americans frequently went to Mexico for sexual alliances with boys ("Vera Cruz" is an easy pun on cruising). Robert may very well love Edna, but when she grabs him aggressively in their last scene together, her gesture tells him that he will have to perform sexually, as a man with a woman. And so (at least according to modern queer readings), if Robert is a gay man, recognizable to other Creoles as gay, he has to run away.

If readers a century ago interpreted Robert as homosexual, no one said so in print, just four years after Oscar Wilde's sensational trial for homosexuality. Possibly the codes for recognizing a gay male character were well known to avant-garde readers in 1899, and they had no need to write down what they already knew.

Meanwhile, our language for recognizing heterosexuality has also shifted. In Kate Chopin's day, readers of *The Awakening* knew exactly what Edna was doing with Alcée Arobin, but a century later, they are less sure. They wonder, for instance, which body parts are involved—but Chopin could not have named the sexual parts of her characters and gotten her book published. She and her contemporaries used literary conventions, just as filmmakers once used symbolic images—

fires flaming up, waves crashing across the sand—as shorthand for sexual acts they could not show. . . .

Kate Chopin's contemporaries would recognize that, in *The Awakening*, Edna has sexual relations with Alcée Arobin on three separate occasions, all indicated by suggestive language and white space. A century later, high school teachers, embarrassed by students' questions and doubtful themselves about literary conventions, often deny that Edna and Arobin actually "do it." They do, and in these chapters: (1) At the end of XXVII: "It was the first kiss of her life to which her nature had really responded. It was a flaming torch that kindled desire." In the white space after that passage, the sex takes place, followed by:

XXVIII

Edna cried a little that night after Arobin left her.

(2) At the end of XXXI: "He did not answer, except to continue to caress her. He did not say good night until she had become supple to his gentle, seductive entreaties." (3) In XXXV: After a night drive with his fast, unmanageable horses, Arobin and Edna arrive at her little house "comparatively early in the evening."

It was late when he left her. It was getting to be more than a passing whim with Arobin to see her and be with her. He had detected the latent sensuality, which unfolded under his delicate sense of her nature's requirements like a torpid, torrid, sensitive blossom.

Works by Kate Chopin

At Fault, 1890

The Awakening, 1899

Bayou Folk, 1894

The Complete Works of Kate Chopin, edited by Per Seyersted, 2 volumes, 1969

A Kate Chopin Miscellany, edited by Per Seyersted and Emily Toth, 1979

A Night in Acadie, 1897

A Vocation and a Voice, edited by Emily Toth, 1991

Annotated Bibliography

Ammons, Elizabeth. *Conflicting Stories: American Women Writers at the Turn into the Twentieth Century*, Oxford University Press, Oxford and New York, 1991, pp. 74–75.

In this extract, Ammons asks the reader to consider the class and race issues in Edna's liberation.

Arnavon, Cyrille. "Introduction" to *Edna* (Paris, 1953), reprinted in *Norton Critical Edition*, 2nd ed., pp. 186–187.

Cyrille Arnavon's comments represent French interest in a neglected American writer. Contemporary critics of Chopin look to Arnavon's translation of the novel and his commentary on it as contributing factors to the achievement of her current stature.

Culley, Margo. "Contexts of *The Awakening*," *Norton Critical Edition: "The Awakening*," W.W. Norton & Company, New York, 1994, pp. 119–121.

In this extract, Culley provides important details for understanding the constraints under which Chopin was writing.

———. "Edna Pontellier: A Solitary Soul," first published in 1976, reprinted in the 2nd edition of the *Norton Critical Edition: "The Awakening*": *Kate Chopin*, ed. Margo Culley, W.W. Norton & Company, New York, 1994, pp. 119–121.

Reminding the reader that Chopin's first title for the novel was *A Solitary Soul*, Culley focuses on the many aspects of solitude—those that are positive and those that are dark and dreadful—that Edna experiences.

Dix, Dorothy. Review in *The Times Picayune*, August 15, 1897.

This commentary, appearing before the publication of *The Awakening*, provides a context for understanding the public commotion generated by Chopin's heroine.

Eble, Kenneth. *Western Humanities Review*, Summer 1956, pp. 261–269; reprinted in *Critical Essays on Kate Chopin*, ed. Alice Hall Petry, 1996, pp. 79–81.

Most commentary on *The Awakening* focuses on its novel ideas and the courage or bad judgment of its author to express them. Here, Eble discusses the author's writing style.

Franklin, Rosemary F. "Edna as Psyche: The Self and the Unconscious," *Approaches to Teaching Chopin's "The Awakening,"* The Modern Language Association of America, New York, 1988, pp. 147–148.

Edna craves romantic fulfillment and awakens to its possibility; in this extract Franklin speculates on its attainability.

Gilbert, Sandra M. *The Kenyon Review* 5, no. 3, Summer 1983; reprinted in *Modern Critical Views: Kate Chopin*, ed., Harold Bloom, Chelsea House Publishers, New York, 1987, pp. 97–99.

Sea, water, and swimming imagery suggest to Gilbert a link between Edna's rebirthing and the mythological figure of Aphrodite.

Kauffmann, Stanley. *The New Republic*, December 3, 1966.

In contrast to Percival Pollard, Stanley Kaufmann values the authentic existential quality of Edna's plight.

Pollard, Percival. *Their Day in Court*, Neale Publishing Company, 1909, pp. 42–44.

Contrasting views on the plight of any character in literature are expected, but it is hard to take seriously Pollard's judgments of Edna because he can find no reason to take her seriously. His comments are useful perhaps because they unwittingly reveal a certain kind of male sensibility. His chiding of the author for revealing "the growth of animalism in a woman" is also interesting as a sign of the times.

Seidel, Kathryn Lee. "Picture Perfect: Painting in *The Awakening*," *Critical Essays on Kate Chopin*, G. K. Hall & Co., New York, 1996, pp. 229–234.

In this essay, Seidel discusses Chopin's heroine, Edna in the larger context of women and art in literature, emphasizing the genuine commitment Edna makes to art "for art's sake."

Solomon, Barbara H. "Characters as Foils to Edna," *Approaches to Teaching Chopin's "The Awakening,"* The Modern Language Association of America, New York, 1988, pp.114–119.

In this extract, Solomon examines the minor characters in the novel whose presence sharply focus the reader on Edna's limitations and possibilities.

Stange, Margit. Johns Hopkins University Press, Baltimore, 1998, pp. 21–35.

Stange takes up the feminist question of who owns a woman that began a century ago with Elizabeth Cady Stanton and others.

Thornton, Lawrence. *American Literature* 52, Duke University Press, March 1980, pp. 50–66; reprinted as *"The Awakening: a Political Romance,"* in *Critical Essays on Kate Chopin*, ed. Petry, G.K. Hall & Co., New York, 1996.

In this extract, Thornton discusses the futility of seeking the kind of success Edna desires.

Toth, Emily. *Unveiling Kate Chopin*, University of Mississippi Press, Jackson, 1999, pp. 211–214.

Toth's recent work on *The Awakening* examines the different causes of misreading for the novel's earliest and most contemporary readers.

Wolff, Cynthia Griffin. "Thanatos and Eros: Kate Chopin's *The Awakening,*" *American Quarterly* 25, no. 4 (October 1973): pp. 452, 453–454.

In this extract, Wolff examines the features of the schizoid personality as it applies to Edna.

Contributors

Harold Bloom is Sterling Professor of the Humanities at Yale University. He is the author of 30 books, including *Shelley's Mythmaking, The Visionary Company, Blake's Apocalypse, Yeats, A Map of Misreading, Kabbalah and Criticism, Agon: Toward a Theory of Revisionism, The American Religion, The Western Canon*, and *Omens of Millennium: The Gnosis of Angels, Dreams, and Resurrection. The Anxiety of Influence* sets forth Professor Bloom's provocative theory of the literary relationships between the great writers and their predecessors. His most recent books include *Shakespeare: The Invention of the Human*, a 1998 National Book Award finalist, *How to Read and Why, Genius: A Mosaic of One Hundred Exemplary Creative Minds, Hamlet: Poem Unlimited, Where Shall Wisdom Be Found?*, and *Jesus and Yahweh: The Names Divine*. In 1999, Professor Bloom received the prestigious American Academy of Arts and Letters Gold Medal for Criticism. He has also received the International Prize of Catalonia, the Alfonso Reyes Prize of Mexico, and the Hans Christian Andersen Bicentennial Prize of Denmark.

Dorothy Dix was the first advice columnist for women. This commentary, appearing before the publication of *The Awakening*, provides a context for understanding the public commotion generated by Chopin's heroine.

Percival Pollard wrote a novel and literary criticism and was interested in expanding the audience for European literature in the United States.

Cyrille Arnavon, critic and translator, prepared the first French edition of *The Awakening*, which stimulated interest in Chopin's initially overlooked work.

Kenneth Eble was a University Professor of English at the University of Utah.

Stanley Kauffmann was drama critic for *The New York Times*, editor-in-chief of Ballantine Books, and literary critic for *The New Republic*.

Cynthia Griffin Wolff taught English at the University of Massachusetts. She is the author of *Samuel Richardson and the Eighteenth-Century Puritan Character*, published in 1972.

Lawrence Thornton teaches literature at the University of California at Los Angeles.

Sandra M. Gilbert was professor of English at Princeton University, co-author of *The Madwoman in the Attic: The Woman Writer and the Nineteenth-Century Literary Imagination*, and the co-editor of *The Norton Anthology of Women's Literature*.

Rosemary F. Franklin taught literature at the University of Georgia.

Barbara H. Solomon taught literature at Iona College.

Elizabeth Ammons is the author of *Conflicting Stories: American Woman Writers at the Turn Into the Twentieth Century*.

Margo Culley is prominent among those responsible for bringing Kate Chopin's work to the high regard it now enjoys. She was professor of English at the University of Massachusetts in Amherst and is the editor of the *Norton Critical Edition: The Awakening*, 2nd edition, 1994.

Kathryn Lee Seidel is professor of English at the University of Central Florida in Orlando. Other works include *The Southern Belle in the American Novel* (1985).

Margit Stange is a contemporary feminist thinker and author.

Emily Toth is the author of *Kate Chopin: A Life of the Author of "The Awakening"* and *Unveiling Kate Chopin* and co-editor of *Private Papers of Kate Chopin*.

Acknowledgments

Cyril Arnavon, "Introduction" to Edna (Paris, 1953, trans. Bjorn Braaten and Emily Toth, in *The Kate Chopin Miscellany*, Per Seyersted and Emily Toth, eds.) Northwestern State University Press, 1979.

Kenneth Eble, *Western Humanities Review*, Summer 1956. Reprinted in *Critical Essays on Kate Chopin*. New York: G. K. Hall, 1996.

Stanley Kauffmann, "The Really Lost Generation," *The New Republic* 155, no. 3 (December 3, 1966): 38.

Cynthia Griffin Wolff, *Thantos and Eros: Kate Chopin's The Awakening*. *American Quarterly* 25: 4 (1973). © The American Studies Association. Reprinted with permission of The Johns Hopkins University Press.

Lawrence Thornton, "The Awakening: A Political Romance," in *American Literature*, volume 52 (March), pp. 55–60. © 1980, Duke University Press. All rights reserved. Used by permission of the publisher.

Sandra M. Gilbert, "The Second Coming of Aphrodite," *The Kenyon Review* 5, no. 3 (Summer 1983). © Kenyon College.

Rosemary F. Franklin, "Edna as Psyche: The Self and the Unconscious," *Approaches to Teaching Chopin's The Awakening*, Modern Language Association of America, 1988. Reprinted by permission.

Barbara H. Solomon, "Patterns that Yield Meaning: Characters as Foils to Edna," *Approaches to Teaching Chopin's The Awakening*, Modern Language Association of America, 1988. Reprinted by permission.

Elizabeth Ammons, "Women of Color in The Awakening," *Conflicting Stories: American Women Writers at the Turn Into the Twentieth Century*, Oxford University Press, 1991. By permission of Oxford University Press, Inc.

Margo Culley, "Editor's Note: Contexts of *The Awakening.*" *From Kate Chopin The Awakening*. Norton Critical Edition. New York: W. W. Norton, 1994.

Kathryn Lee Seidel, "Picture Perfect: Painting in *The Awakening.*" From *Critical Essays on Kate Chopin*. New York: G. K. Hall, 1996.

Margit Stange, *Personal Property: Wives, White Slaves, and the Market in Women*, pp. 21–22, 24, 25, 35, 143–144. © 1998 The Johns Hopkins University Press. Reprinted with permission of The Johns Hopkins University Press.

Emily Toth, "The Awakening," *Unveiling Kate Chopin*, University Press of Mississippi, 1999. Used by permission of University Press of Mississippi.

Index